## My Hands

My hands tremble
As I sign my naturalization papers
Making me a Canadian citizen
And Canada my final resting place.


*TAKEO NAKANO*
*Translated from the Japanese*
*by Robert Y. Kadoguchi*

Cover illustration: Normand Cousineau
Design: Wycliffe Smith

ISBN: 0-921156-10-3

Copyright· © 1989 Rubicon Publishing Inc., Oakville, Ontario

Canadian Cataloguing in Publication Data
Main entry under title:

Between worlds

ISBN: 0-921156-10-3

1. Canadian prose literature (English) - Minority authors.* 2. Canadian prose literature (English) - 20th century.* 3. Minorities - Canada - Literary collections. I. Goh, Maggie. II. Stephenson, Craig.

PS8235.M56B47 1989        C810'.8'0054
C89-094914-X             PR9194.5.M56B47 1989

# Between Worlds

EDITED BY

MAGGIE GOH

•

CRAIG STEPHENSON

RUBICON PUBLISHING INC.

# Table of Contents

▼▼▼▼▼▼▼▼▼▼▼▼▼▼▼▼▼▼▼▼▼▼▼▼▼▼▼▼

| Selection | Author | Page |
| :--- | :--- | :--- |
| • • • • • • • • | • • • • • • • | • • • • • |
| My Hands  (Poetry) | Takeo Nakano | |

## Sojourners

| | | |
| :--- | :--- | :--- |
| Tao Te Ching #80  (Poetry) | Lao Tzu | |
| √ Exiled From Paradise  (Non-fiction) | Eva Hoffman | 3 |
| Departure  (Fiction) | Matilde Torres | 6 |
| ✓ Leaving This Island Place  (Fiction) | Austin Clarke | 9 |
| Sojourners  (Non-fiction) | Annie Dillard | 18 |

## Between Worlds

| | | |
| :--- | :--- | :--- |
| The Laundress  (Poetry) | Einar Pall Jonsson | |
| Urashima the Fisherman  (Fiction) | Royall Tyler | 25 |
| Ice Bangles  (Fiction) | Nazneen Sadiq | 29 |
| √ The Jade Peony  (Fiction) | Wayson Choy | 35 |
| Nocturne  (Non-fiction) | Mario Duliani | 44 |
| The Japanese-Canadian Dilemma  (Non-fiction) | Joy Kogawa | 49 |
| ✓✓ "I'm Not Racist, But..."  (Non-fiction) | Neil Bissoondath | 61 |
| ✓ The Man From Mars  (Fiction) | Margaret Atwood | 64 |
| The Nun Who Returned to Ireland  (Fiction) | Roch Carrier | 85 |

▼▼▼▼▼▼▼▼▼▼▼▼▼▼▼▼▼▼▼▼▼▼▼▼▼▼▼▼▼▼▼▼

| Selection | Author | Page |
|-----------|--------|------|
| •••••••• | •••••• | ••••• |

## Building All Over Again

| | | |
|---|---|---|
| Advice to the Young  (Poetry) | Miriam Waddington | |
| I'm Just Me: Adrienne Clarkson  (Non-fiction) | Maggie Goh | 91 |
| Black Like Me  (Non-fiction) | Fil Fraser | 101 |
| Rebirth  (Fiction) | Pablo Urbanyi | 111 |
| A Boat Girl Grows Up  (Non-fiction) | Barry Came | 119 |
| The Management of Grief  (Fiction) | Bharati Mukherjee | 123 |

# *Introduction*

■

There is a well-known story about a young protagonist who journeys from his village to a magic kingdom, marries into a royal family, and lives happily in his new home for three years, at which point he is suddenly overwhelmed by a longing to see his parents and his ancestral village. His wife and in-laws advise him that such a return is a grave mistake, a destructive temptation, but the young man feels compelled to go back.

Almost every culture has its version of this tragic theme of estrangement, of rootlessness, of the planet Earth as "a hard land of exile in which we are all sojourners," as Annie Dillard observes in an appropriately titled essay.

This collection of short stories and essays offers some fresh renderings of this theme from the context of the immigrant experience. The collection is Canadian (with the exception of the Dillard essay and the Japanese folktale). In practical terms, this simply means that one of the landscapes in each story is Canada. How Canada as setting affects the outcomes is worth pondering.

The anthology is divided into three sections, each centred on an image that is examined from different perspectives. The first section explores the expectations and fears of those poised between departure from the old world and arrival in the new world. The heartfelt question, "Where is my home?" informs the second section, wherein the writers consider the blessings and the curses of the immigrant's double-vision of "home." The final section asks if there are ways to construct meaning out of this dilemma, to redefine "home," and to even celebrate this paradox of double vision.

*Between Worlds* is not a title we have been comfortable with. At best, it promises a healthy tension between memories of a distant homeland and a strange new world of dreams. At worst, as in the folktale, it connotes getting stuck, being nowhere, or maybe even being pulled apart. The writers in this collection continually remind us how risky it all is, how their people could just as easily be defeated as be victorious in their confrontations with this tension. The writers speak with a freshness, a directness, and a tenacity that inspire confidence. The excitement we wish to share with you comes not from happy resolutions but from the strength of the voices and the visions.

*Maggie Goh*      *Craig Stephenson*

# Sojourners

*Tao Te Ching # 80*

*Exiled From Paradise*

*Departure*

*Leaving This Island Place*

*Sojourners*

# *T*ao *T*e *C*hing

■

L     A     O     T     Z     U

If a country is governed wisely,
its inhabitants will be content.
They enjoy the labour of their hands
and don't waste time inventing
labour-saving machines.
Since they dearly love their homes,
they aren't interested in travel.
There may be a few wagons and boats,
but these don't go anywhere.
There may be an arsenal of weapons,
but nobody ever uses them.
People enjoy their food,
take pleasure in being with their families,
spend weekends working in their gardens,
delight in the doings of the neighbourhood.
And even though the next country is so close
that people can hear its roosters crowing and its dogs
barking,
they are content to die of old age
without ever having gone to see it.

*Translated by Stephen Mitchell*

# *E*xiled From Paradise

■

E  V  A     H  O  F  F  M  A  N

*I*t is April 1959, I'm standing at the railing of the *Batory's* upper deck, and I feel that my life is ending. I'm looking out at the crowd that has gathered on the shore to see the ship's departure from Gdynia - a crowd that, all of a sudden, is irrevocably on the other side - and I want to break out, run back, run toward the familiar excitement, the waving hands, the exclamations. We can't be leaving all this behind - but we are. I am thirteen years old, and we are emigrating. It's a notion of such crushing, definitive finality that to me it might as well mean the end of the world.

My sister, four years younger than I, is clutching my hand wordlessly; she hardly understands where we are, or what is happening to us. My parents are highly agitated; they had just been put through a body search by the customs police, probably as the farewell gesture of anti-Jewish harassment. Still, the officials weren't clever enough, or suspicious enough, to check my sister and me - lucky for us, since we

■ ■ ■ ■ ■ ■ ■ ■ ■ ■ ■ ■ ■ ■ ■ ■ ■ ■ ■ ■ ■ ■

Eva Hoffman was born in Cracow, Poland, in 1946. When she was thirteen, she moved to Canada with her family. In her book, *Lost in Translation*, she reflects on her experiences as a Canadian immigrant. She now lives in New York, and is an editor of *The New York Times Book Review*.

▼▼▼▼▼▼▼▼▼

are both carrying some silverware we were not allowed to take out of Poland in large pockets sewn onto our skirts especially for this purpose, and hidden under capacious sweaters.

When the brass band on the shore strikes up the jaunty mazurka rhythms of the Polish anthem, I am pierced by a youthful sorrow so powerful that I suddenly stop crying and try to hold still against the pain. I desperately want time to stop, to hold the ship still with the force of my will. I am suffering my first, severe attack of nostalgia, or *tesknota* - a word that adds to nostalgia the tonalities of sadness and longing. It is a feeling whose shades and degrees I'm destined to know intimately, but at this hovering moment, it comes upon me like a visitation from a whole new geography of emotions, an annunciation of how much an absence can hurt. Or a premonition of absence, because at this divide, I'm filled to the brim with what I'm about to lose - images of Cracow, which I loved as one loves a person, of the sun-baked villages where we had taken summer vacations, of the hours I spent poring over passages of music with my piano teacher, of conversations and escapades with friends. Looking ahead, I come across an enormous, cold blankness - a darkening, an erasure, of the imagination, as if a camera eye has snapped shut, or as if a heavy curtain has been pulled over the future. Of the place where we're going - Canada - I know nothing. There are vague outlines of half a continent, a sense of vast spaces and little habitation. When my parents were hiding in a branch-covered forest bunker during the war, my father had a book with him called *Canada Fragrant with Resin* which, in his horrible confinement, spoke to him of majestic wilderness, of animals roaming without being pursued, of freedom. That is partly why we are going there, rather than to Israel, where most of our Jewish friends have gone. But to me, the word "Canada" has ominous echoes of the "Sahara." No, my mind rejects the idea of being taken there, I don't want to be pried out of my childhood, my pleasures, my safety, my hopes for becoming a pianist. The *Batory* pulls away, the foghorn emits its lowing, shofar sound, but my being is engaged in a stubborn refusal to move. My parents put their hands on my shoulders consolingly; for a moment, they allow themselves to acknowledge that there's pain in this departure, much as they wanted it.

Many years later, at a stylish party in New York, I met a woman who told me that she had had an enchanted childhood. Her father was a highly positioned diplomat in an Asian country, and she had lived surrounded by sumptuous elegance, the courtesy of servants, and the delicate advances of older men. No wonder, she said, that when this part of her life came to an end, at age thirteen, she felt she had been exiled from paradise, and had been searching for it ever since.

No wonder. But the wonder is what you can make a paradise out of. I told her that I grew up in a lumpen apartment in Cracow, squeezed into three rudimentary rooms with four other people, surrounded by squabbles, dark political rumblings, memories of wartime suffering, and daily struggle for existence. And yet, when it came time to leave, I, too, felt I was being pushed out of the happy, safe enclosures of Eden.

*From*
Lost in Translation
*by Eva Hoffman*
*( © 1989).*
*Published by E. P. Dutton.*

# *Departure*

■

M A T I L D E     T O R R E S

*T*he lounge of the airport of Fiumicino was full of passengers. The long-awaited moment of departure was beside me, winked at me, yet I was afraid of reaching it, touching it.

I was not unused to this kind of sensation. Always, in the past, I had set myself a goal, worn myself out getting there and, when it would have been enough to stretch out my hand to reach it, I would put off the realization for another time. For example, when I had to take examinations in the courses at the Faculty of Medicine, I would study all the material industriously, but leave out the last three or four pages. As I was completing my work, I was overcome by a powerful feeling which mastered me and made me leave it. I was aware of the lack of logic in such thoughts, but in spite of my best efforts, I could not manage to drive these quirks from my consciousness.

Curious about them, I asked for an explanation from a psychologist friend with whom I happened to share a train compartment on the Rome-Avezzano line.

■ ■ ■ ■ ■ ■ ■ ■ ■ ■ ■ ■ ■ ■ ■ ■ ■ ■ ■ ■ ■ ■ ■

Matilde Gentile Torres was born in Tagliacozzo, Italy and studied medicine at the University of Rome. Her novel, *La Dottoressa di Cappadocia*, was published in Rome. She emigrated to Canada with her husband in 1977 and now lives in Toronto where she practises medicine.

"The explanation is simple enough," he told me. "With your behaviour, you are trying to translate into practical terms a rather common psychological situation. You are unconsciously led to identify the end of the task or the outcome of an undertaking with the 'finishing' of life. From the correspondence of the two concepts 'finish'-'death', arises the unpleasant association which you have attributed to final acts. To avoid this you put off every finality, in an unconscious attempt to escape death, the absolute 'conclusion', the sum of all the little deaths which accumulate as we live."

"I didn't know I was so sick," I muttered sadly.

"On the contrary! You love life to such a degree that you wish to postpone death!"

"I love life, I love life," I repeated to myself as I sought Vincenzo's hand.

More was given to me, Vincenzo hugged me and looked into my eyes with an intense expression, to inspire me with courage.

Suddenly the metallic voice of the loudspeaker announced, "Travellers leaving for Toronto with Alitalia are requested to go to the departure gate."

We rose and slowly walked to the exit. My legs were wooden and my heart was skipping beats.

The day was splendid, the sky a clear blue with perfect visibility. In the passenger-transport bus we remained in the embrace, without saying a word, for the whole distance to the runway. We went up the stairway to the airplane, the stewardess met us with her mechanical smile and showed us to our places. I closed my eyes, leaned back against the headrest and felt his hand tightly clasp mine. Now we were ready to take off: into the blue sky, into the future which smiled towards us. A new life which only we two had the right to lead.

"Passengers are requested to fasten their seatbelts," the stewardess told us.

The plane began to move, accelerating along the runway until it reached take-off speed. Finally we left the earth!

From above, Rome appeared to me in all its incomparable beauty: the witness to thousands of years of civilization lay below me. The Tyrrhenian Sea washed the beach of Ostia which I had always considered dirty and noisy. Now as I was losing it, it seemed marvellous: it sparkled blue and laughing under the sun, furrowed with billowing whitecaps.

Suddenly I had the sensation that the airplane had stopped in mid-air, attracted to the earth by a mysterious magnetic force. I had to free myself and dissolve the bonds which still bound me to my native land. "Rome..., unequalled, splendid Rome..., I beseech you..., let me go with him..., I love him!"

At that instant the airplane began to gain altitude as it went into its climbing phase, and shortly after we passed through a barrier of clouds which obscured the earth. I noticed a pain in my chest: I had accumulated another little death. "*Alea jacta est*," I said to myself, "the die is cast." I had cut the umbilical cord which bound me to Italy, the "mother country of human civilization." I had annihilated myself in order to rise again in another dimension, in the infinite blue sky, above a froth of clouds and with hope in my heart that beyond the ocean I would find liberty, justice, peace and the happiness I dreamed of. In that moment of exaltation, I had forgotten that, as Goldoni said: "All the world is one country and everywhere mankind is the same."

*Translated by*
*Ann Cameron Burroni*

▼▼▼▼▼▼▼▼▼

# Leaving This Island Place

■

## A U S T I N    C L A R K E

The faces at the grilled windows of the parish almshouse were looking out, on this hot Saturday afternoon, on a world of grey-flannel and cricket and cream shirts, a different world, as they had looked every afternoon from the long imprisonment of the wards. Something in those faces told me they were all going to die in the almshouse. Standing on the cricket field I searched for the face of my father. I knew he would never live to see the sun of day again.

It is not cricket, it is leaving the island that makes me think about my father. I am leaving the island. And as I walk across the green playing field and into the driveway of the almshouse, its walkway speckled with spots of tar and white pebbles, and walk right up to the white spotless front of the building, I know it is too late now to think of saving him. It is too late to become involved with this dying man.

In the open verandah I could see the men, looking half-alive and half-

■ ■ ■ ■ ■ ■ ■ ■ ■ ■ ■ ■ ■ ■ ■ ■ ■ ■ ■ ■ ■
Austin Clarke was born in the Barbados in 1934 and moved to Canada in 1955 to study at the University of Toronto. He is a writer, freelance broadcaster, producer, founding member of the Writer's Union of Canada, and a professor of literature. An acknowledged spokesperson for the black community in Toronto, he most recently published a collection of short stories, *Nine Men Who Laughed*.

dead, lying on the smudged canvas cots that were once white and cream as the cricketers' clothes, airing themselves. They have played, perhaps, in too many muddy tournaments, and are now soiled. But I am leaving. But I know before I leave there is some powerful tug which pulls me into this almshouse, grabbing me and almost swallowing me to make me enter these doors and slap me flat on the sore-back canvas cot beside a man in dying health. But I am leaving.

"You wasn't coming to visit this poor man, this poor father o' yourn?" It is Miss Brewster, the head nurse. She knew my father and she knew me. And she knew that I played cricket every Saturday on the field across the world from the almshouse. She is old and haggard. And she looks as if she has looked once too often on the face of death; and now she herself resembles a half-dead, dried-out flying fish, wrapped in the grease-proof paper of her nurse's uniform. "That man having fits and convulsions by the hour! Every day he asking for you. All the time, day in and day out. And you is such a poor-great, high-school educated bastard that you now acting *too proud* to come in here, because it is a almshouse and not a *private ward*, to see your own father! And you didn' even have the presence o' mind to bring along a orange, not even one, or a banana for that man, *your father!*"

She was now leading me through a long dark hallway, through rows of men on their sides, and some on their backs, lying like soldiers on a battlefield. They all looked at me as if I was dying. I tried to avoid their eyes, and I looked instead at their bones and the long fingernails and toenails, the thermometers of their long idle illness. The matted hair and the smell of men overdue for the bed-pan: men too weary now to raise themselves to pass water even in a lonely gutter. They were dying slowly and surely, for the almshouse was crowded and it did not allow its patients to die too quickly. I passed them, miles out of my mind: the rotting clothes and sores, men of all colours, all ages, dressed like women in long blue sail-cloth-hard shirts that dropped right down to the scales on their toothpick legs. One face smiled at me, and I wondered whether the smile meant welcome.

"Wait here!" It was Miss Brewster again who had spoken. She opened the door of a room and pushed me inside as you would push a small boy into the headmaster's office for a caning; and straightway the smell of stale urine and of sweat and feces whipped me in the face. When the door closed behind me I was alone with the dead, with the smells of the almshouse.

I am frightened. But I am leaving. I find myself thinking about the trimmed sandwiches and the whiskey-and-sodas waiting for me at the farewell party in honour of my leaving. Something inside me is saying I should pay some respect in my thoughts for this man, this dying man. I opened my eyes and thought of Cynthia. I thought of her beautiful face beside my father's face. And I tried to hold her face in the hands of my mind, and I squeezed it close to me and kept myself alive with the living outside world of cricket and cheers and "tea in the pavilion". There is death in this room and I am inside it. And Cynthia's voice is saying to me, Run run run! back through the smells, through the fallen lines of the men, through the front door and out into the green sunlight of the afternoon and the cricket and shouts; out into the applause.

"That's he laying-down there. Your father," the voice said. It was Miss Brewster. She too must have felt the power of death in the room, for she spoke in a whisper.

This is my father: more real than the occasional boundary hit by the cricket bat and the cheers that came with the boundary only. The two large eyeballs in the sunset of this room are my father.

"Boy?" It was the skeleton talking. I am leaving. He held out a hand to touch me. Dirt was under his fingernails like black moons. I saw the hand. A dead hand, a dirty hand, a hand of quarter-moons of dirt under the claws of its nails. ("You want to know something, son?", my godmother told me long ago. "I'll tell you something. That man that your mother tell you to call your father, he isn't your father, in truth. Your mother put the blame of your birth on him because once upon a time, long long ago in this island, that man was a man.")

I do not touch the hand. I am leaving this place.

And then the words, distant and meaningless from this departure of love because they came too late, began to turn the room on a side. Words and words and words. He must have talked this way each time he heard a door open or shut; or a footstep. ". . . is a good thing you going away, son, a good thing. I hear you going away, and that is a good thing . . .because I am going away . . .from this place . . . Miss Brewster, she . . . but I am sorry . . . cannot go with you. . . ." (Did my mother hate this man so much to drive him here? Did she drive him to such a stick of love that it broke his heart; and made him do foolish things with his young life on the village green of cricket near his house, that made him the playful enemy of Barrabas the policeman, whose delight, my godmother told me, was to drag my father the captain of the village team away drunk from victory and pleasure to throw him into the crowded jail to make him slip on the cold floor fast as a new cricket pitch with vomit . . . ("And it was then, my child, after all those times in the jail, that your father contract that sickness which nobody in this village don't call by name. It is so horrible a sickness.") . . . and I remember now that even before this time I was told by my mother that my father's name was not to be mentioned in her house which her husband made for me as my step-father. And she kept her word. For eighteen years. For eighteen years, his name was never mentioned; so he had died before this present visit. And there was not even a spasm of a reminiscence of his name. He was dead before this. But sometimes I would risk the lash of her hand and visit him, in his small shack on the fringe of Rudders Pasture where he lived out the riotous twenty-four years of middle life. ("Your mother never loved that bastard," my godmother said.) But I loved him, in a way. I loved him when he was rich enough to give me two shillings for a visit, for each visit. And although my mother had said he had come, "from no family at-all, at-all", had had "no background", yet to me in those laughing days he held a family circle of compassion in his heart. I see him now, lying somewhere on a cot, and I know I am leaving this island. In those days of cricket when I visited him, I visited him in his house: the pin-up girls of the screen, white and naked; and the photographs of black women he had taken with a box camera (because "Your father is some kind o' genius, but in this island we call him a blasted madman, but he may be a real genius"), black women always dressed in their Sunday-best after church, dressed in too much clothes, and above them all, above all those pin-ups and photographs, the photographs of me, caught running in a record time, torn from the island's newspapers. And there was one of me he had framed, when I passed my examinations at Harrison College.

And once, because in those days he was my best admirer, I gave him a silver cup which I had won for winning a race in a speed which no boy had done in twenty-five years, at the same school, in the history of the school. And all those women on the walls, and some in real life, looking at me, and whispering under their breath so I might barely hear it, "That's his *son* !"; and some looking at me as if I had entered their bedroom of love at the wrong moment of hectic ecstasy; and he, like a child caught stealing, would hang his father's head in shame and apologize for them in a whisper, and would beg the women in a loud voice, "You don't see I am with *my son* ? You can't behave yourself in his presence?" And once, standing in his house alone, when he went to buy a sugar cake for me, I was looking at the photograph of a naked woman on the wall and my eyes became full of mists and I saw coming out of the rainwater of vision my mother's face, and her neck and her shoulders and her breasts and her navel. And I shut my eyes tight, tight, tight and ran into him returning with the sugar cake and ran screaming from his house. That was my last visit. This is my first visit after that. And I am leaving this island place. After that last visit I gave myself headaches wondering if my mother had gone to his shack before she found herself big and heavy with the burden of me in her womb. ("Child, you have no idea what he do to that poor pretty girl, your mother, that she hates his guts even to this day!") . . . and the days at Harrison College when the absence of his surname on my report card would remind me in the eyes of my classmates that I might be the best cricketer and the best runner, but that I was after all, among this cream of best blood and brains, only a bas-) ". . . this island is only a place, one place," his voice was saying. "The only saving thing is to escape." He was a pile of very old rags thrown around a stunted tree. Then he was talking again, in a new way. "Son, do not leave before you get somebody to say a prayer for me . . . somebody like Sister Christopher from the Nazarene Church . . . ."

But Sister Christopher is dead. Dead and gone five years now, "When she was shouting at the Lord one night at a revival", my godmother said.

"She's dead."

"*Dead* ?"

"Five years."

"But couldn' you still ask her to come, ask Miss Christo, Sister Christopher to come. . . ."

There is no point listening to a dying man talk. I am going to leave. No point telling him that Sister Christopher is alive, because he is beyond that, beyond praying for, since he is going to die and he never was a Catholic. And I am going to leave. For I cannot forget the grey-flannel and the cream of the cricket field just because he is dying, and the sharp smell of the massage and the cheers of the men and women at the tape, which I have now made a part of my life. And the Saturday afternoon matinees with the wealthy middle-class girls from Queen's College, wealthy in looks and wealthy in books, with their boyfriends the growing-up leaders of the island. Forget all that? And forget the starched white shirt and the blue-and-gold Harrison College tie? Forget all this because a man is dying and because he tells you he is going to die?

Perhaps I should forget them. They form a part of the accident of my life, a life which - if there were any logic in life - ought to have been spent in the gutters round the Bath Corner, or in some foreign white woman's rose garden, or fielding tennis balls in the Garrison Savannah Tennis Club where those who played tennis could be bad tennis players but had to be white.

Let him die. I am leaving this island place. And let him die with his claim on my life. And let the claim be nailed in the coffin, which the poor authorities for the poor will authorize out of plain dealboard, without a minister or a prayer. And forget Sister Christopher who prefers to testify and shout on God; and call somebody else, perhaps, more in keeping with the grey-flannel and the cream of the cricket field and Saturday afternoon walks in the park and matinees at the Empire Theatre. Call a canon. Call a canon to bury a pauper, call a canon to bury a pauper, ha-ha-haaaa! . . . .

Throughout the laughter and the farewell speeches and the drinks that afternoon, all I did hear was the slamming of many heavy oak doors of the rectory when I went to ask the canon to bury the pauper. And I tried to prevent the slamming from telling me what it was telling me:

that I was out of place here, that I belonged with the beginning in the almshouse. Each giggle, each toast, each rattle of drunken ice cubes in the whirling glass pointed a finger back to the almshouse. "Man, you not drinking?" a wealthy girl said. "Man, what's wrong with you, at all?" And Joan Warton said, "But wait, look this lucky bastard though, saying he going up in Canada to university! Boy, you real lucky, in truth. I hear though that up there they possess some real inferior low-class rum that they does mix with water. Yak-yak-yak! From now on you'd be drinking Canadian rum-water, so drink this Bajan rum, man. We paying for this, yuh know!" I was leaving. I was thinking of tomorrow, and I was climbing the BOAC gang-plank on the plane bound for Canada, for hope, for school, for glory; and the sea and the distance had already eased the pain of conscience; and there was already much sea between me and the cause of conscience . . . .

And when the party was over, Cynthia was with me on the sands of Gravesend Beach. And the beach was full of moonlight and love. There was laughter too; and the laughter of crabs scrambling among dead leaves and skeletons of other crabs caught unawares by someone running into the sea. And there was a tourist ship in the outer harbour. "Write! write, write, write, write me everyday of the week, every week of the year, and tell me what Canada is like, and think of me always, and don't forget to say nice things in your letters, and pray for me every night. And write poems, love poems like the ones you write in the college magazine; and when you write don't send the letters to the Rectory, because father would, well . . . send them to Auntie's address. You understand? You know how ministers and canons behave and think. I have to tell father, I have to tell him I love you, and that we are getting married when you graduate. And I shall tell him about us ... when you leave tomorrow." Watching the sea and the moonlight on the sea; and watching to see if the sea was laughing; and the scarecrows of masts on the fishing boats now lifeless and boastless, taking a breather from the depths and the deaths of fishing; and the large incongruous luxury liner drunk-full of tourists. And all the time Cynthia chatting and chattering, ". . . but we should have got married, even secretly and eloped somewhere, even to Trinidad, or even to Tobago. Father won't've known, and won't've liked it, but we would've been married

. . . .Oh hell, man! this island stifles me, and I wish I was leaving with you. Sometimes I feel like a crab in a crab hole with a pile o' sand in front. . . ."

"Remember how we used to build sandcastles on bank holidays?"

"And on Sundays, far far up the beach where nobody came . . . ."

"Cynthia?"

"Darling?"

"My Old Man, my Old Man is dying right now. . . ."

"You're too philosophical! Anyhow, where? Are you kidding? I didn' even know you had an Old Man." And she laughs.

"I was at the almshouse this afternoon, before the party."

"Is he really in the almshouse?"

"St Michael's almshouse, near . . . ."

"You must be joking. You *must* be joking!" She turned her back to me, and her face to the sea. "You aren't pulling my leg, eh?" she said. And before I could tell her more about my father, who he was, how kind a man he was, she was walking from me and we were in her father's Jaguar and speeding away from the beach.

And it is the next day, mid-morning, and I am sitting in the Seawell Airport terminal, waiting to be called to board the plane. I am leaving. My father, is he dead yet? A newspaper is lying on a bench without a man, or woman. Something advises me to look in the obituary column and see if . . . . But my mother had said, as she packed my valises, making sure that the fried fish was in my briefcase which Cynthia had bought for me as a going-away present, my mother had said, "Look, boy, leave the dead to live with the blasted dead, do! Leave the dead in this damn islan' place!"

And I am thinking now of Cynthia who promised ("I promise, I promise, I promise. Man, you think I going let you leave this place, *leave Barbados*? and I not going be there at the airport?") to come to wave goodbye, to take a photograph waving goodbye from the terminal and the plane, to get her photograph taken for the social column waving good-bye at the airport, to kiss, to say goodbye and promise return in English, and say "*au revoir*" in French because she was the best student in French at Queen's College.

A man looks at the newspaper, and takes it up, and gives it to a man loaded-down as a new-traveller for a souvenir of the island. And the friend wraps two large bottles of Goddards Gold Braid rum in it, smuggling the rum and the newspaper out of the island, in memory of the island. And I know I will never find out how he died. Now there are only the fear and the tears and the handshakes of other people's saying good-bye and the weeping of departure. "Come back real soon again, man!" a fat, sweating man says, "and next time I going take you to some places that going make your head *curl*! Man, I intend to show you the whole islan', and give you some dolphin steaks that is more bigger than the ones we eat down in Nelson Street with the whores last night!" An old woman, who was crying, was saying goodbye to a younger woman who could have been her daughter, or her daughter-in-law, or her niece. "Don't take long to return back, child! Do not tarry too long. Come back again soon . . .and don't forget that you was borned right here, pon this rock, pon this island. This is a good decent island, so return back as soon as you get yuh learning, come back again soon, child . . . ."

The plane is ready now. And Cynthia is not coming through the car park in her father's Jaguar. She has not come, she has not come as she promised. And I am leaving the island.

Below me on the ground are the ants of people, standing at an angle, near the terminal. And I can see the architect-models of houses and buildings, and the beautiful quiltwork patches of land under the plough . . . and then there is the sea, and the sea, and then the sea.

▼▼▼▼▼▼▼▼▼▼

# Sojourners

∎

A  N  N  I  E       D  I  L  L  A  R  D

*I*f survival is an art, then mangroves are artists of the beautiful: not only that they exist at all - smooth-barked, glossy-leaved, thickets of lapped mystery - but that they can and do exist as floating islands, as trees upright and loose, alive and homeless on the water.

I have seen mangroves, always on tropical ocean shores, in Florida and in the Galápagos. There is the red mangrove, the yellow, the button, and the black. They are all short, messy trees, waxy-leaved, laced all over with aerial roots, woody arching buttresses, and weird leathery berry pods. All this tangles from a black muck soil, a black muck matted like a mud-sopped rag, a muck without any other plants, shaded, cold to the touch, tracked at the water's edge by herons and nosed by sharks.

It is these shoreline trees which, by a fairly common accident, can become floating islands. A hurricane flood or a riptide can wrest a tree

■ ■ ■ ■ ■ ■ ■ ■ ■ ■ ■ ■ ■ ■ ■ ■ ■ ■ ■ ■ ■ ■ ■

Annie Dillard was born in Pittsburgh, Pennsylvania. She has been described as "a fine wayfarer, one who travels light, reflective and alert to the shrines and holy places." Her best known book, for which she won the Pulitzer Prize, is *Pilgrim At Tinker Creek* ; her most recent and most personal is *An American Childhood*. She now lives in Middletown, Connecticut with her husband.

from the shore, or from the mouth of a tidal river, and hurl it into the ocean. It floats. It is a mangrove island, blown.

There are floating islands on the planet; it amazes me. Credulous Pliny described some islands thought to be mangrove islands floating on a river. The people called these river islands *the dancers*, "because in any consort of musicians singing, they stir and move at the stroke of the feet, keeping time and measure."

Trees floating on rivers are less amazing than trees floating on the poisonous sea. A tree cannot live in salt. Mangrove trees exude salt from their leaves; you can see it, even on shoreline black mangroves, as a thin white crust. Lick a leaf and your tongue curls and coils; your mouth's a heap of salt.

Nor can a tree live without soil. A hurricane-born mangrove island may bring its own soil to the sea. But other mangrove trees make their own soil - and their own islands - from scratch. These are the ones which interest me. The seeds germinate in the fruit on the tree. The germinated embryo can drop anywhere - say, onto a dab of floating muck. The heavy root end sinks; a leafy plumule unfurls. The tiny seedling, afloat, is on its way. Soon aerial roots shooting out in all directions trap debris. The sapling's networks twine, the interstices narrow,and water calms in the lee. Bacteria thrive on organic broth; amphipods swarm. These creatures grow and die at the trees' wet feet. The soil thickens, accumulating rainwater, leaf rot, seashells, and guano; the island spreads.

More seeds and more muck yield more trees on the new island. A society grows, interlocked in a tangle of dependencies. The island rocks less in the swells. Fish throng to the backwaters stilled in snarled roots. Soon, Asian mudskippers - little four-inch fish - clamber up the mangrove roots into the air and peer about from periscope eyes on stalks, like snails. Oysters clamp to submerged roots, as do starfish, dog whelk, and the creatures that live among tangled kelp. Shrimp seek shelter there, limpets a holdfast, pelagic birds a rest.

And the mangrove island wanders on, afloat and adrift. It walks teetering and wanton before the wind. Its fate and direction are random. It may bob across an ocean and catch on another mainland's shores. It may starve or dry while it is still a sapling. It may topple in a storm, or pitchpole. By the rarest of chances, it may stave into another mangrove island in a crash of clacking roots, and mesh. What it is most likely to do is drift anywhere in the alien ocean, feeding on death and growing, netting a makeshift soil as it goes, shrimp in its toes and terns in its hair.

We could do worse.

I alternate between thinking of the planet as home - dear and familiar stone hearth and garden - and as a hard land of exile in which we are all sojourners. Today I favour the latter view. The word "sojourner" occurs often in the English Old Testament. It invokes a nomadic people's sense of vagrancy, a praying people's knowledge of estrangement, a thinking people's intuition of sharp loss: "For we are strangers before thee, and sojourners, as were all our fathers: our days on the earth are as a shadow, and there is none abiding."

We don't know where we belong, but in times of sorrow it doesn't seem to be here, here with these silly pansies and witless mountains, here with sponges and hard-eyed birds. In times of sorrow the innocence of the other creatures - from whom and with whom we evolved - seems a mockery. Their ways are not our ways. We seem set among them as among lifelike props for a tragedy - or a broad lampoon - on a thrust rock stage.

It doesn't seem to be here that we belong, here where space is curved, the earth is round, we're all going to die, and it seems as wise to stay in bed as budge. It is strange here, not quite warm enough, or too warm, too leafy, or inedible, or windy, or dead. It is not, frankly, the sort of home for people one would have thought of - although I lack the fancy to imagine another.

The planet itself is a sojourner in airless space, a wet ball flung across nowhere. The few objects in the universe scatter. The coherence of matter dwindles and crumbles toward stillness. I have read, and repeated, that our solar system as a whole is careering through space toward a point east of Hercules. Now I wonder: what could that possibly mean, east of Hercules? Isn't space curved? When we get "there," how will our course change, and why? Will we slide down the universe's inside arc like mud slung at a wall? Or what sort of welcoming shore is this east of Hercules? Surely we don't anchor there, and disembark, and sweep into dinner with our host. Does someone cry, "Last stop, last stop"? At any rate, east of Hercules, like east of Eden, isn't a place to call home. It is a course without direction; it is "out." And we are cast.

These are enervating thoughts, the thoughts of despair. They crowd back, unbidden, when human life as it unrolls goes ill, when we lose control of our lives or the illusion of control, and it seems that we are not moving toward any end but merely blown. Our life seems cursed to be a wiggle merely, and a wandering without end. Even nature is hostile and poisonous, as though it were impossible for our vulnerability to survive on these acrid stones.

Whether these thoughts are true or not I find less interesting than the possibilities for beauty they may hold. We are down here in time, where beauty grows. Even if things are as bad as they could possibly be, and as meaningless, then matters of truth are themselves indifferent; we may as well please our sensibilities and, with as much spirit as we can muster, go out with a buck and wing.

The planet is less like an enclosed spaceship - spaceship earth - than it is like an exposed mangrove island beautiful and loose. We the people started small and have since accumulated a great and solacing muck of soil, of human culture. We are rooted in it; we are bearing it with us across nowhere. The word "nowhere" is our cue: the consort of musicians strikes up, and we in the chorus stir and move and start twirling our hats. A mangrove island turns drift to dance. It creates its own soil as it goes, rocking over the salt sea at random, rocking day and night and round the sun, rocking round the sun and out toward east of Hercules.

▼▼▼▼▼▼▼▼▼▼

# Between Worlds

*The Laundress*

*Urashima the Fisherman*

*Ice Bangles*

*The Jade Peony*

*Nocturne*

*The Japanese-Canadian Dilemma*

*'I'm Not Racist, But...'*

*The Man From Mars*

*The Nun Who Returned to Ireland*

▼▼▼▼▼▼▼▼▼▼▼▼▼▼▼▼▼▼▼▼▼▼▼

# The Laundress

■

## EINAR PALL JONSSON

She worked as a housemaid, then as a laundress
in small town Winnipeg, full of emigres speaking
every language except her own:  she was Icelandic
and as she worked she sang the old Icelandic hymns
and songs:  the songs had all her joy, they brought
all her peace.  She kept reaching for the language
that got lost in her life.  She could never speak it
again, though it always measured her breath.

Late one summer, as she lay dying, she sang again
the Icelandic hymns, sang in her mother tongue,
an other tongue for us; and as we lay her
in a foreign grave, we, who know no Icelandic,
who know then almost nothing of what she loved
and lived by, say our prayers over her in English.

*Translated from the Icelandic*
*by Michael Patrick O'Connor*
*and Thorvaldur Johnson*

# Urashima the Fisherman

■

R  O  Y  A  L  L      T  Y  L  E  R

*Y*oung Urashima lived in Tango province, in the village of Tsutsugawa. One day in the fall of 477 (it was Emperor Yuryaku's reign), he rowed out alone on the sea to fish. After catching nothing for three days and nights, he was surprised to find that he had taken a five-coloured turtle. He got the turtle into the boat and lay down to sleep.

When the turtle changed into a dazzlingly lovely girl, the mystified Urashima asked her who she was.

"I saw you here, alone at sea," she answered with a smile, "and I wanted so much to talk to you! I came on the clouds and the wind."

"But where did you come from, then, on the clouds and wind?"

"I'm an Immortal and I live in the sky. Don't doubt me! Oh, be kind and speak to me tenderly!"

Urashima understood she was divine, and all his fear of her melted away.

■ ■ ■ ■ ■ ■ ■ ■ ■ ■ ■ ■ ■ ■ ■ ■ ■ ■ ■ ■

Royall Tyler was born in England in 1936 and has lived in the United States, Canada, France, and Japan. After studying Japanese Literature at Harvard and Columbia universities, he taught Japanese language and literature at the University of Toronto as well as in the United States. Since 1984, he has been living in Norway.

▼ ▼ ▼ ▼ ▼ ▼ ▼ ▼ ▼

"I'll love you as long as the sky and earth last," she promised him, "as long as there's a sun and a moon! But tell me, will you have me?"

"Your wish is mine," he answered. "How could I not love you?"

"Then lean on your oars, my darling, and take us to my Eternal Mountain!"

She told him to close his eyes. In no time they reached a large island with earth like jade. Watchtowers on it shone darkly, and palaces gleamed like gems. It was a wonder no eye had seen and no ear had ever heard tell of before.

They landed and strolled on hand in hand to a splendid mansion, where she asked him to wait; then she opened the gate and went in. Seven young girls soon came out of the gate, telling each other as they passed him that he was Turtle's husband; and eight girls who came after them told each other the same. That was how he learned her name.

He mentioned the girls when she came back out. She said the seven were the seven stars of the Pleiades, and the eight the cluster of Aldebaran. Then she led him inside.

Her father and mother greeted him warmly and invited him to sit down. They explained the difference between the human and the divine worlds, and they let him know how glad this rare meeting between the gods and a man had made them. He tasted a hundred fragrant delicacies and exchanged cups of wine with the girl's brothers and sisters. Young girls with glowing faces flocked to the happy gathering, while the gods sang their songs sweetly and clearly and danced with fluid grace. The feast was a thousand times more beautiful than any ever enjoyed by mortals in their far-off land.

Urashima never noticed the sun going down, but as twilight came on the Immortals all slipped away. He and the maiden, now alone, lay down in each other's arms and made love. They were man and wife at last.

For three years he forgot his old life and lived in paradise with the Immortals. Then one day he felt a pang of longing for the village where he had been born and the parents he had left behind. After that, he missed them more each day.

"Darling," said his wife, "you haven't looked yourself lately. Won't you tell me what's wrong?"

"They say the dying fox turns toward his lair and the lesser man longs to go home. I'd never believed it, but now I know it's true."

"Do you want to go back?"

"Here I am in the land of the gods, far from all my family and friends. I shouldn't feel this way, I know, but I can't help being homesick for them. I want so much to go back and see my mother and father!"

His wife brushed away her tears. "We gave ourselves to each other forever!" she lamented. "We promised we'd be as true as gold or the rocks of the mountains! How could a little homesickness make you want to leave me?"

They went for a walk hand in hand, sadly talking it all over. Finally they embraced, and when they separated their parting was sealed.

Urashima's parents-in-law were sad to see him go. His wife gave him a jeweled box. "Dearest," she said, "if you don't forget me and find you want to come back, then grip this box hard. But you mustn't open it, ever."

He got into his boat and they told him to close his eyes. In no time he was at Tsutsugawa, his home. The place looked entirely different. He recognized nothing there at all.

"Where's Urashima's family - Urashima the fisherman?" he asked a villager.

"Who are you?" the villager answered. "Where are you from? Why are you looking for a man who lived long ago? Yes, I've heard old people mention someone named Urashima. He went out alone on the sea and never came back. That was three hundred years ago. What do you want with him now?"

Bewildered, Urashima roamed the village for ten days without finding any sign of family or old friends. At last he stroked the box his divine lady had given him and thought of her; then, forgetting his recent promise, he opened it. Before his eyes her fragrant form, borne by the clouds and the wind, floated up and vanished into the blue sky. He understood he had disobeyed her and would never see her again. All he could do was gaze after her, then pace weeping along the shore.

When he dried his tears, he sang about her far, cloud-girdled realm. The clouds, he sang, would bring her the message of his love. Her sweet voice answered him, across the vastness of the sky, entreating him never to forget her.  Then a last song burst from him as he struggled with his loss: "My love, when after a night of longing, day dawns and I stand at my open door, I hear far-off waves breaking on the shores of your paradise!"

If only he hadn't opened that jeweled box, people have said since, he could have been with her again.  But the clouds hid her paradise from him and left him nothing but his grief.

▼▼▼▼▼▼▼▼▼

# *Ice Bangles*

■

## N A Z N E E N   S A D I Q

*T*hey danced in a semi-circle on the wooden dais. The plates of henna paste studded with burning candles dipped and twirled with them. It was a family tradition to choose the most beautiful women for the dance. A way of saying to the in-laws, "Look how wonderful we are". Naila danced with her sisters and cousins in a city in northern Pakistan, the hypnotic tattoo of the long wooden drum quickening her steps to keep up with the others, the melody, almost forgotten, resurfacing, coiling around her like the scent of roses and jasmine.

As she spun around, the carousel of colours and faces swam before her: her two-year-old Canadian daughter squirming in the arms of an older family member. The smiling faces of her aunts and uncles packed into the enormous marquee. Her brother, the bridegroom, seated in the centre flashing her a look which said "What a carnival". His bride-to-be, a saffron-shrouded figure seated on a cushioned stool. Bent and motionless, with coral-tinted toes peeping out of her gilt sandals, she

Nazneen Sadiq was born in Kashmir in 1944, and came to Canada when she was twenty. Along with *Ice Bangles*, she has also written a children's book called *Camels Can Make You Homesick and Other Stories*.

▼▼▼▼▼▼▼▼▼

observed the festivities through a saffron coloured veil. The clusters of women with embroidered silks and wedding jewelry. Her father immaculately clad in a three-piece English wool suit ushering people in. Stouffville, Ontario, became a memory put on hold, unreal and thousands of miles away.

"Your brother getting married, please attend," had been the words of the telegram which had arrived in Canada three weeks ago. It was followed a week later by another cable which read "Bring clothes and jewelry". That cable was from her mother, a subtle reminder that she was not to arrive as a Canadian, whatever that was, but a daughter of the house. She had dashed off to Georg Jensen on Bloor Street and bought a tulip-shaped silver candle-holder as a wedding gift. This was her way of expressing her independence from the system she had left. The sleek and unadorned sensuous lines of the piece were a contrast to the embossed and heavily cut silver the family would give to her brother and his wife.

When she landed in Islamabad, the capital of Pakistan, holding her daughter and the Canadian wedding present, she was pressed into the melee of the wedding. She was taken off to meet her brother's fiancee, a slight petite woman with masses of black hair and the dark complexion of a southerner. She did not come up to her family's standard of the lighter-complexioned beauties, but was connected to a powerful family. It wasn't really her father who mattered but her grandfather, a wiry autocratic man who controlled the largest government financial institution. She was informed by her mother that she had to go and pay her respects to him as well. Preferably before she met the bride-to-be. She fought her mother on that score, and decided that she didn't care whose grand-daughter she was. What mattered was that she was going to marry her brother.

Fatimeh sat in a large room with her trousseau littered around her, peering myopically through oversized spectacles. When Naila came up to greet her, she removed the glasses and tossed her head back defiantly. Her eyes widened imperiously, and the cloud of hair shifted like a silken armour around her. They observed each other warily, as strangers who had parts assigned to them without their permission.

Naila was embarrassed herself, because she knew that waiting outside the room were clusters of people who would want to know immediately if she approved of her sister-in-law. She also knew that this approval was based solely on the colour of the bride's skin. Standing before her was a woman free and strong enough to choose her own husband, but hopelessly tangled in a subtle web of discrimination which Pakistanis practised with shocking malice. The fair-skinned northerners had practised for centuries the same discrimination which their British masters had been accused of. Her mother, who had hoped secretly for a Kashmiri wife for her only son, had been cheated.

Fatimeh had a Master's degree from the University and studied French at the Alliance Française. She had exerted the strength of her personality and her slightly comic stance towards life to charm her brother. Despite this, she needed the weight of her grandfather's status, a necklace of dazzling value and a trousseau of three hundred accessorized outfits to compensate for her tawny skin. Naila's charming devil-may-care brother, who had spent two years in London rounding off his engineering degree with training in computers, had come home only to reject the fair-skinned candidates lined up for him. He had settled instead for the slightly over-aged and physically under-endowed Fatimeh.

She had already caught the scent of disparaging comments made by distant relatives who had hoped that her brother would marry one of their daughters.

"Welcome to the family," she said to Fatimeh, who gazed at her quite serenely.

"I'm so fed up with all these people in the house, do you have a cigarette?" said her brand new sister-in-law.

"Oh, of course." Naila laughed at this surprising request.

"Don't tell your brother, he doesn't know as yet."

"Of course not, I promise," she said hurriedly.

"I've heard so much about you," said Fatimeh, smoke streaming through her nostrils, looking like a fallen angel.

"So have I," she blurted back.

"Your fair brother marrying such a dark woman?" came the sardonic reply.

"Not at all." The protest leapt out of Naila.

"Wait till you see me dressed up," informed her sister-in-law, a rich womanly smile stretching across her flawless skin.

"I like you already," she replied.

"I was going to write to you," said Fatimeh.

"I would have loved hearing from you," she replied, relieved that the blunt exchange was over.

"I wanted a *Better Homes and Gardens* cook-book from Canada."

"I wish I'd known, I bought you a candle holder," she replied, and they both laughed, cook-book tying them, holding them together in an arc of laughter and a new friendship.

"Well, well, what do you think?" Her cousin's sharp eyes skewered her.

"I like her very much," she replied.

"May God shower his blessings on this marriage," intoned her cousin seeking refuge behind a show of piety.

The horse was a pure white Arabian and its groom tagged close to the procession. Her brother had mounted the horse just before the gates of the bride's house. He was dressed in a formal brocade tunic and tight silken trousers. The wedding turban completely veiled with flowers and tinsel hid his entire face. Seated behind him was a young cousin who was dressed as a replica of the groom. The little boy jabbed at the horse's flank with his turned up brocade slippers, and the skittish Arabian would have dumped his cargo on the gravel-strewn drive, if the groom had not murmured warning commands to him.

Naila and her other two sisters held the reins on either side, and she thought of Kathleen in Stouffville and how she would have loved the extravagant spectacle of a Pakistani wedding, particularly one which had revived dying customs to satisfy Eastern showmanship. Her well-educated liberal parents had organized a pageant. Her brother had parked his brand new Volkswagen, purchased during his stay in London, and mounted a horse.

Waiting in the gardens of the sprawling mansion ahead of them, two thousand wedding guests chatted and mingled. The bride would appear as soon as the bridegroom was seated under the canopied dais. Sitting with her brother on the dais and waiting for the bride, Naila thought of the solemn Anglican wedding she had attended in Toronto, but there was a common link. The expectant hush which awaited the first glimpse of the bride was the same.

Fatimeh was led up to the dais by solid phalanx of her female relatives. She appeared in their jewelled and sequinned midst as a glittering icon. She had to be supported because she was almost bent double from the collective weight of her jewelry and clothes. When she climbed the dais and sat next to her brother, she settled herself statuesquely, straightening her shoulders. A collar of oversized turquoise encircled her slender throat, and a filigree web studded with rubies and pearls spilled over her chest. She later found out that a third of her father's pension fund had been handed over to the jeweller who had made the ruby set.

Her sister-in-law's face, dusted with gold powder, was luminous and breathtaking. She had fulfilled her promise of being something other than a dark complexioned woman. Fatimeh shot an amused glance at her before she lowered her gilt-dusted eyelids to assume the pose of modesty. Her head bent, and the wedding veil covered her face, locking her into a private and unreachable space. Yet in the split-second moment of the glance directed at her, Fatimeh had revealed her own contempt for the traditions of her culture.

"Well, she certainly looks beautiful," whispered her elder sister, something reluctant and grudging lacing its way through the compliment. She turned around to face her sister, who wore massive gold earrings and had her three daughters ringed around her feet like puppies. There was a gleam of infuriating superiority razor-sharp in her eyes. It was a quality Naila had never quite noticed before. She could picture her quietly confident sister-in-law wreaking havoc with the ill-placed smugness which emanated from her sister. There were undercurrents which leapt from the concealed grudging note of her sister's voice. She found them mildly offensive, and a surge of protectiveness for Fatimeh coursed through her.

Her mother came and cupped Fatimeh's face in both hands and kissed her forehead. The official stamp of approval spread like a ripple in the sea of people around the bridal dais, and the stampede towards the bridal couple began. Each guest would congratulate the bride and she would raise a hand with the thumb tucked in and 'salaam' them. In return, a roll of currency would be pressed into her hand. Each amount was noted and gathered by a family member standing behind the couple. Fatimeh sat like a robot, the hand rising and falling with precision for over three hours. The pile of bank notes overflowed from beaded handbags. She turned around and whispered to her brother that they needed an oversized garbage bag. He rolled his eyes and gave her a droll smile. She thought about the band of kids who prowled through her neighbourhood in Stouffville at Halloween dragging pillowcases and garbage bags to collect candy.

Balancing a plate of food in hand and disentangling the hands of her daughter from the pleats of her sari, she found herself viewing everything around her with new eyes. She felt as though she had stumbled on the set of some theatrical production. Everything was larger than life. The silken clothes were too shiny, and the twenty-two carat gold jewelry was too yellow. The wedding buffet tables with mountains of pilaf and tureens of seasoned meats stretched in unending lines. The abundance was oppressive, but the faces around her remained comforting.

Peeping over the concrete walls of the enormous grounds were clusters of children, eyes peering through dishevelled hair bunched around gaunt faces. These were the children of the domestic servants, who wanted to see the goings-on of the privileged throng inside. She was conscious for the first time of social divisions and found them disturbing. Five years of living in Canada had awakened a social conscience which emerged with the embarrassment of adolescent acne.

She had been breathless with excitement before she had left Canada. Her elder sister's wedding years ago held memories of childish excesses: a surfeit of sweets, and handfuls of money which came her way for being the bride's little sister. Naila remembered prancing before her mother's dressing table in clothes stitched for the wedding.

She had wanted to touch a familiar part of her life again, and experience well-known emotions. Now she felt as though she was a voyeur, observing unknown, and feeling a detachment that was as alien as it was terrifying.

*From*
Ice Bangles
*by Nazneen Sadiq*
*(© 1988).*
*Published by James Lorimer and Company, Publishers.*

▼▼▼▼▼▼▼▼

# The Jade Peony

■

# W A Y S O N    C H O Y

hen Grandmama died at 83 our whole household held its breath. She had promised us a sign of her leaving, final proof that her present life had ended well. My parents knew that without any clear sign, our own family fortunes could be altered, threatened. My stepmother looked endlessly into the small cluttered room the ancient lady had occupied. Nothing was touched; nothing changed. My father, thinking that a sign should appear in Grandmama's garden, looked at the frost-killed shoots and cringed: *no, that could not be it.*

My two older teenage brothers and my sister, Liang, age 14, were embarrassed by my parents' behaviour. What would all the white people in Vancouver think of us? We were Canadians now, *Chinese-Canadians,* a hyphenated reality that my parents could never accept. So it seemed, for different reasons, we all held our breath waiting for *something.*

■ ■ ■ ■ ■ ■ ■ ■ ■ ■ ■ ■ ■ ■ ■ ■ ■ ■ ■ ■ ■ ■ ■

Wayson Choy is a native of Vancouver. Born in 1939, he attended Gladstone High School and the University of British Columbia. Choy's work has appeared in *Prism, River's Bend Review,* and *Best American Short Story.* He now resides in Toronto, where he is a Teaching Master at Humber College of Applied Arts and Technology.

▼ ▼ ▼ ▼ ▼ ▼ ▼ ▼ ▼

I was eight when she died. For days she had resisted going into the hospital . . . *a cold, just a cold* . . . and instead gave constant instruction to my stepmother and sister on the boiling of ginseng roots mixed with bitter extract. At night, between wracking coughs and deadly silences, Grandmama had her back and chest rubbed with heated camphor oil and sipped a bluish decoction of an herb called Peacock's Tail. When all these failed to abate her fever, she began to arrange the details of her will. This she did with my father, confessing finally: "I am too stubborn. The only cure for old age is to die."

My father wept to hear this. I stood beside her bed; she turned to me. Her round face looked darker, and the gentleness of her eyes, the thin, arching eyebrows, seemed weary. I brushed the few strands of gray, brittle hair from her face; she managed to smile at me. Being the youngest, I had spent nearly all my time with her and could not imagine that we would ever be parted. Yet when she spoke, and her voice hesitated, cracked, the sombre shadows of her room chilled me. Her wrinkled brow grew wet with fever, and her small body seemed even more diminutive.

"I - I am going to the hospital, Grandson." Her hand reached out for mine. "You know, Little Son, whatever happens I will never leave you." Her palm felt plush and warm, the slender, old fingers boney and firm, so magically strong was her grip that I could not imagine how she could ever part from me. Ever.

Her hands *were* magical. My most vivid memories are of her hands: long, elegant fingers, with impeccable nails, a skein of fine, barely-seen veins, and wrinkled skin like light pine. Those hands were quick when she taught me, at six, simple tricks of juggling, learnt when she was a village girl in Southern Canton; a troupe of actors had stayed on her father's farm. One of them, "tall and pale as the whiteness of petals," fell in love with her, promising to return. In her last years his image came back like a third being in our two lives. He had been magician, acrobat, juggler, and some of the things he taught her she had absorbed and passed on to me through her stories and games. But above all, without realizing it then, her hands conveyed to me the quality of their love.

Most marvellous for me was the quick-witted skill her hands revealed in making windchimes for our birthdays: windchimes in the likeness of her lost friend's only present to her, made of bits of string and scraps, in the centre of which once hung a precious jade peony. This wondrous gift to her broke apart years ago, in China, but Grandmama kept the jade pendant in a tiny red silk envelope, and kept it always in her pocket, until her death.

These were not ordinary, carelessly made chimes, such as those you now find in our Chinatown stores, whose rattling noises drive you mad. But making her special ones caused dissension in our family, and some shame. Each one that she made was created from a treasure trove of glass fragments and castaway costume jewellery, in the same way that her first windchime had been made. The problem for the rest of the family was in the fact that Grandmama looked for these treasures wandering the back alleys of Keefer and Pender Streets, peering into our neighbours' garbage cans, chasing away hungry, nervous cats and shouting curses at them.

"All our friends are laughing at us!" Older Brother Jung said at last to my father, when Grandmama was away having tea at Mrs. Lim's.

"We are not poor," Oldest Brother Kiam declared, "yet she and Sek-Lung poke through those awful things as if-" he shoved me in frustration and I stumbled against my sister, "-they were beggars!"

"She will make Little Brother crazy!" Sister Liang said. Without warning, she punched me sharply in the back; I jumped. "You see, look how *nervous* he is!"

I lifted my foot slightly, enough to swing it back and kick Liang in the shin. She yelled and pulled back her fist to punch me again. Jung made a menacing move towards me.

"Stop this, all of you!" My father shook his head in exasperation. How could he dare tell the Grand Old One, his aging mother, that what was somehow appropriate in a poor village in China, was an abomination here. How could he prevent me, his youngest, from accompanying her? If she went walking into those alley-ways alone she could well be attacked by hoodlums. "She is not a beggar looking for food. She is searching for - for . . . ."

My stepmother attempted to speak, then fell silent. She, too, seemed perplexed and somewhat ashamed. They all loved Grandmama, but she was *inconvenient*, unsettling.

As for our neighbours, most understood Grandmama to be harmlessly crazy, others that she did indeed make lovely toys but for what purpose? Why? they asked, and the stories she told me, of the juggler who smiled at her, flashed in my head.

Finally, by their cutting remarks, the family did exert enough pressure so that Grandmama and I no longer openly announced our expeditions. Instead, she took me with her on "shopping trips," ostensibly for clothes or groceries, while in fact we spent most of our time exploring stranger and more distant neighbourhoods, searching for splendid junk: jangling pieces of a vase, cranberry glass fragments embossed with leaves, discarded glass beads from Woolworth necklaces . . . . We would sneak them all home in brown rice sacks, folded into small parcels, and put them under her bed. During the day when the family was away at school or work, we brought them out and washed every item in a large black pot of boiling lye and water, dried them quickly, carefully, and returned them, sparkling, under her bed.

Our greatest excitement occurred when a fire gutted the large Chinese Presbyterian Church, three blocks from our house. Over the still-smoking ruins the next day, Grandmama and I rushed precariously over the blackened beams to pick out the stained glass that glittered in the sunlight. Small figure bent over, wrapped against the autumn cold in a dark blue quilted coat, happily gathering each piece like gold, she became my spiritual playmate: "There's a good one! *There!*"

Hours later, soot-covered and smelling of smoke, we came home with a Safeway carton full of delicate fragments, still early enough to steal them all into the house and put the small box under her bed. "These are special pieces," she said, giving the box a last push, "because they come from a sacred place." She slowly got up and I saw, for the first time, her hand begin to shake. But then, in her joy, she embraced me. Both of our hearts were racing, as if we were two dreamers. I buried my face in her blue quilt, and for a moment, the whole world seemed silent.

"My juggler," she said, "he never came back to me from Honan...
perhaps the famine . . . ." Her voice began to quake. "But I shall have
my sacred windchime . . . I shall have it again."

One evening, when the family was gathered in their usual places in
the parlour, Grandmama gave me her secret nod: a slight wink of her
eye and a flaring of her nostrils. There was *trouble* in the air. Supper
had gone badly, school examinations were due, father had failed to meet
an editorial deadline at the *Vancouver Chinese Times*. A huge sigh came
from Sister Liang.

"But it is useless this Chinese they teach you!" she lamented, turning
to Stepmother for support. Silence. Liang frowned, dejected, and went
back to her Chinese book, bending the covers back.

"Father," Oldest Brother Kiam began, waving his bamboo brush in
the air, "you must realize that this Mandarin only confuses us. We are
Cantonese speakers . . . ."

"And you do not complain about Latin, French or German in your
English school?" Father rattled his newspaper, signal that his patience
was ending.

"But, Father, those languages are *scientific*," Kiam jabbed his brush
in the air. "We are now in a scientific, logical world."

Father was silent. We could all hear Grandmama's rocker.

"What about Sek-Lung?" Older Brother Jung pointed angrily at me.
"He was sick last year, but this year he should have at least started
Chinese school, instead of picking over garbage cans!"

"He starts next year," Father said, in a hard tone that immediately
warned everyone to be silent. Liang slammed her book.

Grandmama went on rocking quietly in her chair. She complimented
my mother on her knitting, made a remark about the "strong beauty"
of Kiam's brushstrokes which, in spite of himself, immensely pleased
him. All this babbling noise was her family torn and confused in a
strange land: everything here was so very foreign and scientific.

The truth was, I was sorry not to have started school the year before.
In my innocence I had imagined going to school meant certain
privileges worthy of all my brothers' and sister's complaints. The fact
that my lung infection in my fifth and sixth years, mistakenly diagnosed
as TB, earned me some reprieve, only made me long for school the

more. Each member of the family took turns on Sunday, teaching me or annoying me. But it was the countless hours I spent with Grandmama that were my real education. Tapping me on my head she would say, "Come, Sek-Lung, we have *our* work," and we would walk up the stairs to her small crowded room. There, in the midst of her antique shawls, the old ancestral calligraphy and multi-coloured embroidered hangings, beneath the mysterious shelves of sweet herbs and bitter potions, we would continue doing what we had started that morning: the elaborate windchime for her death.

"I can't last forever," she declared, when she let me in on the secret of this one. "It will sing and dance and glitter," her long fingers stretched into the air, pantomiming the waving motion of her ghost chimes; "My spirit will hear its sounds and see its light and return to this house and say goodbye to you."

Deftly she reached into the Safeway carton she had placed on the chair beside me. She picked out a fish-shape amber piece, and with a long needle-like tool and a steel ruler, she scored it. Pressing the blade of a cleaver against the line, with the fingers of her other hand, she lifted up the glass until it cleanly snapped into the exact shape she required. Her hand began to tremble, the tips of her fingers to shiver, like rippling water.

"You see that, Little One?" She held her hand up. "That is my body fighting with Death. He is in this room now."

My eyes darted in panic, but Grandmama remained calm, undisturbed, and went on with her work. Then I remembered the glue and uncorked the jar for her. Soon the graceful ritual movements of her hand returned to her, and I became lost in the magic of her task: she dabbed a cabalistic mixture of glue on one end and skillfully dropped the braided end of a silk thread into it. This part always amazed me: the braiding would slowly, *very* slowly, *unknot*, fanning out like a prized fishtail. In a few seconds the clear, homemade glue began to harden as I blew lightly over it, welding to itself each separate silk strand.

Each jam-sized pot of glue was precious; each large cork had been wrapped with a fragment of pink silk. I remember this part vividly, because each cork was treated to a special rite. First we went shopping in the best silk stores in Chinatown for the perfect square of silk she required. It had to be a deep pink, a shade of colour blushing toward red. And the tone had to match - as closely as possible - her precious jade carving, the small peony of white and light-red jade, her most lucky possession. In the centre of this semi-translucent carving, no more than an inch wide, was a pool of pink light, its veins swirling out into the petals of the flower.

"This colour is the colour of my spirit," she said, holding it up to the window so I could see the delicate pastel against the broad strokes of sunlight. She dropped her voice, and I held my breath at the wonder of the colour. "This was given to me by the young actor who taught me how to juggle. He had four of them, and each one had a centre of this rare colour, the colour of Good Fortune." The pendant seemed to pulse as she turned it: "Oh, Sek-Lung! He had white hair and white skin to *his toes! It's true*, I saw him bathing." She laughed and blushed, her eyes softened at the memory. The silk had to match the pink heart of her pendant: the colour was magical for her, to hold the unravelling strands of her memory . . . .

It was just six months before she died that we really began to work on her windchime. Three thin bamboo sticks were steamed and bent into circlets; 30 exact lengths of silk thread, the strongest kind, were cut and braided at both ends and glued to stained glass. Her hands worked on their own command, each hand racing with a life of its own: cutting, snapping, braiding, knotting . . . . Sometimes she breathed heavily and her small body, growing thinner, sagged against me. *Death*, I thought, *He is in this room*, and I would work harder alongside her. For months Grandmama and I did this every other evening, a half dozen pieces each time. The shaking in her hand grew worse, but we said nothing. Finally, after discarding hundreds, she told me she had the necessary 30 pieces. But this time, because it was a sacred chime, I would not be permitted to help her tie it up or have the joy of raising it. "Once tied," she said, holding me against my disappointment, "not even I can raise it. Not a sound must it make until I have died."

"What will happen?"

"Your father will then take the centre braided strand and raise it. He will hang it against my bedroom window so that my ghost may see it, and hear it, and return. I must say goodbye to this world properly or wander in this foreign devil's land forever."

"You can take the streetcar!" I blurted, suddenly shocked that she actually meant to leave me. I thought I could hear the clear-chromatic chimes, see the shimmering colours on the wall: I fell against her and cried, and there in my crying I knew that she would die. I can still remember the touch of her hand on my head, and the smell of her thick woolen sweater pressed against my face. "I will always be with you, Little Sek-Lung, but in a different way . . . you'll see."

Months went by, and nothing happened. Then one late September evening, when I had just come home from Chinese School, Grandmama was preparing supper when she looked out our kitchen window and saw a cat - a long, lean white cat - jump into our garbage pail and knock it over. She ran out to chase it away, shouting curses at it. She did not have her thick sweater on and when she came back into the house, a chill gripped her. She leaned against the door: "That was not a cat," she said, and the odd tone of her voice caused my father to look with alarm at her. "I can not take back my curses. It is too late." She took hold of my father's arm: "It was all white and had pink eyes like sacred fire."

My father started at this, and they both looked pale. My brothers and sister, clearing the table, froze in their gestures.

"The fog has confused you," Stepmother said. "It was just a cat."

But Grandmama shook her head, for she knew it was a sign. "I will not live forever," she said. "I am prepared."

The next morning she was confined to her bed with a severe cold. Sitting by her, playing with some of my toys, I asked her about the cat.

"Why did father jump at the cat with the pink eyes? He didn't see it, you did."

"But he and your mother know what it means."

"What?"

"My friend, the juggler, the magician, was as pale as white jade, and he had pink eyes." I thought she would begin to tell me one of her stories, a tale of enchantment or of a wondrous adventure, but she only paused to swallow; her eyes glittered, lost in memory. She took my hand, gently opening and closing her fingers over it. "Sek-Lung," she sighed, "*he* has come back to me."

Then Grandmama sank back into her pillow and the embroidered flowers lifted to frame her wrinkled face. I saw her hand over my own, and my own began to tremble. I fell fitfully asleep by her side. When I woke up it was dark and her bed was empty. She had been taken to the hospital and I was not permitted to visit.

A few days after that she died of the complications of pneumonia. Immediately after her death my father came home and said nothing to us, but walked up the stairs to her room, pulled aside the drawn lace curtains of her window and lifted the windchimes to the sky.

I began to cry and quickly put my hand in my pocket for a handkerchief. Instead, caught between my fingers, was the small, round firmness of the jade peony. In my mind's eye I saw Grandmama smile and heard, softly, the pink centre beat like a beautiful, cramped heart.

# *N*octurne

■

M A R I O    D U L I A N I

*I*t is today the 29th., the penultimate day of this month of June that began with manifest apprehension among all Italians in Canada. The attitude taken by the Government of Rome with regard to Paris and London was becoming more threatening every day. The Italians approached each other on the street with anxious looks.

-Do you think that Mussolini will declare war?

-Against whom?

-Against France and England . . . because of the Axis Pact . . . .

-That could never be! At the time of the assassination of Chancellor Dollfuss, Mussolini mobilized two armies against Germany. In '14, he was an ardent supporter of the Italian intervention against Germany and Austria. Not long ago he was saying . . . .

-Yes, yes, that's all well and good, but all indications become increasingly alarming. They have already suspended liner service between Naples and New York. The fascist press, that follows party orders, is becoming more and more aggressive toward France . . . . We

■ ■ ■ ■ ■ ■ ■ ■ ■ ■ ■ ■ ■ ■ ■ ■ ■ ■ ■ ■ ■

Mario Duliani was born in 1885 and worked in Montreal as a newspaper editor, journalist, and dramatist until his death in 1964. He was interned from 1940 to 1943 when Italy was allied with Germany during the second world war. He published an autobiographical novel in French and Italian.

hear nothing but talk of partial mobilization, no doubt a prelude to general mobilization . . . . Look! Italy counts eight million infantrymen, thousands of planes, numerous armoured divisions . . . .

-But don't you see that Germany and Russia are united by a secret treaty . . . . Hitler may come to an agreement with Stalin. Mussolini will never comply with him!

And so it went, for hours and hours, as all eventualities were considered, weighed, reckoned, while the hearts of those Italians swung back and forth, from doubt to hope, from fear to a fleeting sense of safety, since each in himself would not have really wanted Italy to change its traditional politics that bound it to France and England, the politics that had permitted a divided people, dominated by foreign powers, to conceive a unity all their own and to fashion a life of prosperity in their own country, in the span of a mere half a century. But despite the arguing, questioning, reasoning, the news from Rome kept getting worse.


Soon they no longer dared voice their thoughts or express their fears. Whatever the outcome, this whole thing was sure to turn into a "dirty affair" for all who, while living in Canada, had shown some ideological or platonic sympathy toward Fascism, since they would become ipso facto enemies!

-What will happen to us? those Italians kept wondering; clearly the decisions of the Government of Rome could not be held as a grievance against them!

Friends, well intentioned or well informed persons, had taken the trouble to warn them:

-Beware! If Mussolini declares war, you run the risk of being interned.

The Italians would answer:

-Why should we be, when we've never done anything against Canada, when our children were born and raised in this country . . . .

-It doesn't matter! they would reply; the laws of war are the laws of war! There'll be Canadians interned in Italy. It is natural that there should be Italians interned in Canada. And so the dialogue pursued.

Even when the Italian insisted on the innocence of his intentions, protesting that he'd never been a spy, nor been in charge of any mission, nor been invested with mandates by the Italian government, still, the inflexibly logical reply of the friend came back: "The laws of war are the laws of war! There will be Canadians interned in Italy. It is natural that there should be Italians interned in Canada!"

We reached thus, Monday, the tenth of June.

In an act of folly, the Government of Rome declared war against France and Great Britain. The die was cast.

In Montreal, the round ups began . . . .

Those who had been pointed out, had to be arrested. And none was spared.

After being detained for two nights and one day in the prison ward of the Provincial Detention Centre, on Wednesday the 12th., we were transported, with armed escort, in buses, to a place a few miles outside Montreal. Here we remained for eighteen days, carefully guarded and well nourished. Finally, yesterday morning, we were broken up into two groups. The first was sent off to a prison and the other, the one to which I belong, boarded a special train that sped toward a destination undisclosed to us.

In fact, at about four o'clock in the evening, our train stopped in the middle of a military camp. Tarpaulin covered trucks were waiting for us. They made us climb into them. Then the long file of vehicles started to move, along a road cut through the forest. The more we advanced the more we sank into the trees . . . . Then, a camp in sight. A few improvised barracks. Barbed wire. Guards. Some other prisoners, Germans, who'd been kept there since September 1939, seemed to be on the look out for our arrival.

At last, here we are in the barracks, in the middle of the night, with this atrocious feeling of being prisoners who knows for how much longer, not knowing what our loved ones might be going through, aware that they will not learn for several days that we're no longer near them, that we will not be able to see them again for some time to come.

This sensation of being astray intensifies, sharpens, tortures.

I find myself suddenly out of breath, my hands clinging to the small frame of the window veiled by a metal grid, and I think that I may never be able to overcome my despair . . . . Then, at the zenith, the sky becomes coloured with a faint glimmer. The thick shadow of the night recomposes itself into a suspicion of forms. Gradually, these forms gather details, take precise shapes. The tree tops draw anew their green embroidery on the immense loom of the celestial vault.

Day has come, clear, clean, cool, pure! And with it the end of the nightmare which few among us were able to elude. And so I try once more to believe in myself, in the future and in the reality of the things that surround me. What I endure is nothing but a parenthesis in my existence, a trial that must be accepted with serenity, firmness, and above all, with resigned patience.

The fatal law that governs the things of this world determines that to each action there corresponds a reaction and that to each adverse event there corresponds a favourable one. The moment when all things will be restored in this world so that the normal course of events may return, will be, for us too, our return to order.

Till then, only patience, patience.

The sound of a bugle, in the distance, calls the reveille.

From all the beds in the cell the men emerge. The interpellations follow. Each one swallows his intimate anguish, not wishing, by a kind of reserve, to appear to be suffering. Words, the pleasantries we sift through a thousand times over, pass from mouth to mouth and surprising as it may seem, make us laugh! Even vulgarities. Whatever it may be. So long as we give the impression of holding on.

Alone or in groups, we go out to wash, each holding the towel, the soap, the toothpaste. We feel the salutary action of the cold water. We dream perhaps, inside ourselves, of having woken up as usual, in our own homes . . . but no one utters a single word. Everyone keeps his jaw locked and feigns to being cheerful. Cheerful, even in these blue uniforms with the large red or white discs drawn on the back, worn by all prisoners, in all the countries of the world, that look like carnival costumes where the clownishness grazes the sinister.

The activities of the day are already planned, assigned, distributed. These men, as a team, will go into the forest to fell trees. Those others, also as a team, will be transported in trucks, to a place fifteen miles from here, to work at the repairs of a bridge. Others will be satisfied by more modest chores. The men of feeble or poor health will go to peel vegetables in the kitchen. A few will do work in the refectory. There are also those who will be in charge, a relatively easy task, of sweeping and washing the barrack-room

Six hundred men, insensibly readapted to a new condition, to a new environment, will resume a seeming rhythm of life. I watch each one moving toward his burden. And I tell myself:

-Courage! Life must be accepted always as it comes . . . .


*Translated by Antonino Mazza*

# The Japanese-Canadian Dilemma

J O Y    K O G A W A

*I*t's Wednesday night, downtown Toronto. Three of us are sitting in a basement room in the dark with our eyes closed. We're holding hands. This is a private hidden thing. We're praying together. Prayer is not something I talk about generally or write about except in my diary. It sounds too much like hocus-pocus. People think of Mackenzie King summoning up ghosts or looking at the hands of a clock to give him direction. He sounds slightly nuts. So do those who pray.

Worship is a primitive impulse. People have always been trying to get to the big picture whether through telescopes and microscopes or the handier lens within. I believe in prayer with my primitive committed heart. There's also doubt. Belief and doubt are both carried here to this basement room.

The three of us are each letting our "stuff" float up through the quiet

■ ■ ■ ■ ■ ■ ■ ■ ■ ■ ■ ■ ■ ■ ■ ■ ■ ■ ■ ■ ■

Joy Kogawa was born in Vancouver in 1935 and lived with her family in a Japanese internment camp in British Columbia during World War II. Best known for her novel *Obasan* which describes these wartime experiences and for her poetry, Kogawa works in support of the Japanese-Canadian community. "We all need to strengthen our capacity to hear one another," she says; "everybody is a minority of some kind."

spaces. I find myself talking about an article for *Toronto Life* that I've been asked to do. I'm blocked. I'm supposed to write about Japanese Canadians and redress. Lord, I'm so tired of being a professional ethnic. There's no peeling off of the skin at 5 o'clock or getting weekends free.

I spoke earlier today with a fellow Japanese Canadian, a Nisei like myself, born in British Columbia. He said there were a lot of people working on redress and he was tired of the whole thing as well.

"You should do more important things," he said.

"You don't think the telling of our story is important?"

There are still many Canadians, politicians included, whose hearts and minds are uninformed about who we are or what was done to us. Surely that lack of information is our responsibility. Forty years ago we were treated as unwanted foreigners in this country. Today, we are still treated as foreigners - by strangers, at parties, in department stores. Bharati Mukherjee found it impossible to stay here in our bureaucratically fuelled grassroots racism and fled to the United States. She said if she'd stayed, she would have had to give up writing and become a political activist.

My friend raised his eyebrows. "Really!" he exclaimed. "I'm surprised. Do you personally experience racism here? You're obviously free to write and say anything you want."

I told him I thought our skin had grown thick in this jab-heavy environment. I asked him what he felt when former prime minister Trudeau went to Japan and apologized there for what was done to Japanese Canadians here. Would he have gone to France to apologize for the wrongs against French Canadians?

"Well," my friend said and shrugged. "Does it really matter? Is anyone suffering because of it?" He was suggesting it was a petty point.

"What do you think about the problems of the Native peoples?" he asked. I admitted there were more urgent issues in today's troubled world than Japanese-Canadian redress. "However every issue has its own legitimacy," I argued. "And more justice here doesn't mean less justice there. What's important to anyone is whatever they care about. Do you care about Japanese Canadians?"

"I don't find them a particularly imaginative group," he said.

"We're like everyone else," I said. His remark reminded me of a familiar old weight, one that I thought I'd put aside in recent months - a feeling something like irritation, or lethargy. I changed the topic. The conversation was beginning to have the texture of many warmed-over interviews - always about Japanese Canadians.

Here in the basement room I tell my prayer group I'm confused about the article request and don't really know what I'm supposed to be doing. We hand it over. Our prayers keep on rambling. We pray for someone who's going in for a serious operation. Then somehow we're talking about Gandhi the man and *Gandhi* the movie and we get on to another area of confusion for me. The movie business. Some people are interested in making a movie of *Obasan*. Business is a world I don't much understand - a world of cactus plants, prickly to the touch, growing, it seems to me, in a desert of mistrust. Caesar reigns in the business desert, claiming what is Caesar's due, for Caesar's short-lived glory. What's the difference between Caesar and a thief? What's the difference between my mistrust of business and the mistrust of Japanese Canadians in the past?

I've said I'm confused so often tonight that I feel embarrassed and expect a certain censure. But censure is the opposite thing to expect from an exercise in prayer. Everything is for handing over. I hand over the movie concern along with the *Toronto Life* article. We pray about our kids. We hand them over too. It feels like a great dumping ground.

Thursday morning and I wake up thinking vaguely that I'll call *Toronto Life* to tell the editors I can't write the article. Every angle I think up leads me to some fellow Japanese Canadian feeling hurt or enraged or envious or fearful. I don't have the necessary freedom to write about us. Of course some people in the community are always suggesting that an article would straighten things out. It would take more than that.

I'm thinking of Earle Birney's poem about Vancouver - how the city lights sparkle from the mountain. From far enough away, the Japanese-Canadian community might look beautiful, but I've been in the back alleys with the garbage pails recently. Horrible hurts happen in an environment of fear. Kindest intentions seen through filters of mistrust are monstrously transformed. It's a place to walk gingerly. Politics is the art of toe-watching and what a tangle of toes and bunions leap about in the microcosm of Japanese-Canadian politics. It's not the most elegant dancing. How much more beautiful we would find ourselves if we could see one another from the perspective of mountain tops. If we could break through our fears

It's 10 o'clock, and I call up a friend - the one who first put the article idea on to boil. I give her my reasons for not doing it. First, I'm tired. I'm worn out by the push-pull in the Japanese-Canadian community. Some people obviously fear a backlash, and having worked so hard to be as invisible as possible, can't bear the limelight. I've met a few whose energy is deep and powerful and who battle "because of the principle of the thing." Some are interested in legal perspectives and confine their involvement to the pen. Some see justice in economic terms alone. Others see money as an undignified and insulting measure of their suffering. One clergyman speaks of forgiveness. Another replies that forgiveness applies to people, not to systems and systems need overhauling. Yet another says that forgiveness is meaningless without repentance and admission of wrong. Some say that the door to these discussions should never have been opened. Others, that the door should never be closed. Some community leaders are accused of militancy and selfishness. Others are accused of selling out, or of using the issue for purely personal political ambitions, or of having no social conscience. Some community members fear that greed or the appearance of greed is the image being created and that our true stories will not receive a sympathetic hearing. Some say there's been sympathy enough and we should get on with all our tomorrows. Some want a full public inquiry of our history in depth and in detail.

I tell my friend that the current tempest in the community teapot will someday be past and that will be the time to write. I can hope that those who now consider me to be their political enemy will change their minds. Things are in such flux and I'm too close to it all. Witnesses are only as good as their vision, I tell her, and I can't see. Besides, print is a solidifier and isn't it wrong, I ask lamely, to solidify what is still flowing along? Isn't the pen easily abused and thereby made an instrument of harm in times of turmoil?

She starts gunning me down. "You don't have to see a *Toronto Life* article as your definitive statement to the Japanese-Canadian community," she says. "That's not who you're primarily speaking to." She tells me she thinks I'm being a coward and that I'm really using all these arguments just to cover up. "You're scared of what people will say," she says. That gets to me.

I try one last shot. I tell her I believe the community needs support and perspective from the outside and that non-Japanese Canadians should take up the task. Someone else should write the article. It's the responsibility of others as much as ours. It's Canada's story.

She says bluntly that others already have and people who are obviously on the inside are obligated to speak up. "Write about the silence and how awful it still is," she says.

I grit my teeth.

"You'll do it," she says.

I don't answer.

"Good," she says, and hangs up.

It's another bulldozing day. I stare out the window and think about how much I hate writing and hate the subject. *The silence and how awful it still is.* There's nothing to eat in the fridge. I should go and look for some background material. Where did I put all those Muriel Kitagawa papers I used for writing my novel? They're probably buried in the basement under all the unpacked boxes of papers from the last move. Funny how Naomi, the narrator in *Obasan*, went to the attic for these papers and I go to the basement.

They're here under the steps in the box at the bottom. Good ol' Muriel. All this stuff from - what was it - seven years ago? Hello again, dear unrelenting ghost. The spirit of Muriel Fujiwara Kitagawa first haunted me through these papers in the Public Archives in Ottawa. She was an activist of the '40s, a young, married woman with a pen, a historian's guide. She wrote letters, poems, short stories, articles, passionate manuscripts, which her husband, Ed, sent to Ottawa's Public Archives. She died before I could meet her.

Some people didn't like her, they tell me. She was not known for diplomacy. In spite of all her trampled toes, Muriel's unpopular courage strides into tomorrow, more surely than the good and squeaky feet of some of her more diplomatic contemporaries.

When I first read her material, I was gripped. I carried her papers through the halls of the Archives, holding back the tears, facing the corners where no one could see me. Sometimes, around midnight, I would sit alone in the huge rooms of tables and let the floodgates loose.

Whatever else Muriel did or didn't do, she did not fail to love Canada and Canadians. There was no other country for her. On page thirty-four of her manuscript titled "Go East," in which she describes some of the agonies of the time when we were being exiled, she writes ". . . even for the bitterest ones, there really was no choice at all, because whatever the provocation, we could not conceive of ourselves as anything but Canadian." Her passionate loyalty, her rage, haven't been left to molder in the grave. A book by Muriel Kitagawa titled *This Is My Own*, edited by Roy Miki of Vancouver, is out this year. What a relief that is. What a cause for celebration.

I do so much wish she were here still, and I wish I'd met her. I wish they could all come back - those passionate Niseis and Isseis who toiled and toiled and toiled till they dropped to prove and overprove that they were worthy of the love of their fellow Canadians. People such as George Tanaka, T. Buck Suzuki, Kunio Shimizu and all the other warriors who have died. What a cloud of unsung heroes surrounds us. Muriel says we "had to choose our allegiance under such stress and strain, under duress." And she believed that "hardships, obstacles, persecutions tend to crystallize the instinctive loyalty . . . ." It's interesting to think of loyalty as crystal - a jewel to cherish and to wear. But loyalty, whether to a person or a community or a country, can be destroyed. What seems marvellous to me about these politically active idealists in our community is that they remained loyal throughout their lives in spite of all the treachery. Such bright uncrushed diamonds.

But I don't know how Muriel and the other leaders coped with the bleatings of the critics in the community - those who are always complaining that the doers are doing too much or not enough, are going too fast or too slow, are being too autocratic or indecisive etc. etc.

Resentments, timidities, criticisms, envies are the plague of insects that anyone who tries to do anything has to face. Maybe Muriel became a fly swatter to survive the mosquito mob.

Addressing the security seekers of her day, she wrote: "Perhaps we want nothing better than to forget the raw wounds of yesterday, to cover the scars with delusions of security, but what was once taken away can be taken again. Who knows but that the next time will be made easier for the plunderers because we shrugged and said: 'Shikata-ga-nai' (it can't be helped)."

Her words still apply. We'd still like to cover our scars with delusions of security. It's so easy to forget that we do not live by bread alone and that the rumblings in our belly are not the best guide. We can become so malnourished, so hungry for spiritual bread that we barely wobble along, hardly knowing the difference between principles of justice and rationalizations for greed, between acts of generosity and acts based on fear.

Some people who remember the '40s say that our community today is reliving the same dynamics that were at work in the past. The terrors have by no means been forgotten. People remember the terrible helplessness, the confusion, the frustration, the conflicting reports, the need to be extra good, quiet and submissive and to pander to authorities. Many of us still believe that if we lie perfectly still and don't rock the boat, the storms will disappear and we'll be safe. The lessons of oppression can remain a lifetime.

At the official level, government taught us our lessons well, labouring to create disunity in the community, to disperse us, to destroy our will, and, toward the end, to provide a "final solution to the Japanese problem" by exiling us.

Cyril Powles, whom I see in church most Sundays, was writing back in the '40s, warning about the potential disaffection of Japanese Canadians unless policies changed. "A problem, sufficiently discouraging before the war, might be rendered practically insoluble," he wrote. It seems reasonable to suppose that if you treat loyal citizens as if they were spies and treacherous traitors, if you imprison them, steal their properties, deprive them of the means to earn their livelihoods, if you take away their rights of citizenship for seven years, if you exile them for no crime

- if you do these despicable things, it seems reasonable to suppose that somewhere down the line problems will arise.

My tolerant friend who advised me to concern myself with more important matters agreed that it was all a terrible thing. "But," he said, "what do you think would have happened to us if we'd fought back?" He shook his head as he answered himself, "We wouldn't be here. We just wouldn't be around. That's how bad it was."

It seems we were lucky that we had some friends. Although the White Canada Association argued that we were completely unassimilable, that each and every one of us was disloyal, that we would be happier out of the country, that we were a menace to working conditions and so on, we had powerful friends who knew better.

Thank God for friends. The Reverend James Finlay, the chairman of the Co-Operative Committee on Japanese Canadians, was a friend of Muriel. His was the home where Ed and Muriel and their family first stayed when they moved to Toronto. With Reverend Hugh MacMillan as executive secretary and Andrew Brewin as legal advisor, the Co-Operative Committee formed a powerful lobby team.

News Bulletin #5 of the Co-Operative Committee describes a conference of an hour and a half with Prime Minister Mackenzie King and Cabinet members on March 26, 1946. The deputation representing the Co-Operative Committee consisted of E.J. Tarr, KC, of Winnipeg; Charles Millard, national director, United Steelworkers of America and executive member of the Canadian Congress of Labour; Andrew Brewin, Hugh MacMillan, David Croll, Liberal MP, and M.J. Coldwell, national leader of the CCF. They were arguing against the deportation and exile of innocent Canadian citizens.

Two days later on March 28, 1946, Kunio Hidaka, executive secretary of the Citizenship Defence Commission, has a fulsome report of the meeting. He describes various reactions by Mr. King and Mr. St. Laurent, minister of justice. While sympathetic to the Co-Operative Committee, they are not willing to withdraw the deportation orders. The Honorable Ian Mackenzie, minister of veterans affairs from British Columbia, calls the efforts of the Co-Operative Committee, "frothy idealism" by persons unable to face "hard realities."

A full two years later, in March, 1948, Jack Scott writes a satirical piece in the *Vancouver Sun* - a dialogue between Goebbels and Hitler in Hell. They're gleefully discussing the good news from Canada that British Columbia Liberal Party members have become their men.

"What a splendid joke!" Hitler says, roaring with laughter.

Goebbels: "Good men. Good men all. And highly respected . . . . Why, one of their leaders - now a senator - swore that he would leave public life if the Japs returned to that coastal strip."

Hitler: "Capital! A man after my own heart. Truly a real senator!"

Goebbels: "A Scotsman, by the way. Name of Mackenzie."

Hitler: "Hoot mon!"

Goebbels: "Ja, Mein Fuehrer, it is just as if you were there in person. A helpless minority used beautifully for political and economic purposes. A forthright stand against a race of a different colour or creed. Just as in our better days. And just think: a whole year ban on them!" (On March 8, 1948, the government announced we would be banned from the B.C. coast for at least another year.)

Hitler: "Ach, Doctor. We are far from dead so long as we have our friends up there."

Goebbels: "Hoot mon, Mein Fuehrer."

I find it not easy to believe, but I'm told that government bureaucrats are not so different today. They are as unimaginative as ever, caring about their jobs, their families, their friends and little else. It's still who you know that counts. And woe to those people who have no one to represent them. I've heard that the same sentiments, the same arrogance and racial contempt that raged upon us in the '40s are still present behind closed doors among senators and Cabinet members. If that is true, we must seek out our Desmond Tutus.

Kunio Hidaka, one of our lifelong warriors, died just this year, the day after I saw him speaking to a public meeting of the National Association of Japanese Canadians. I still mourn him. I hope his idealism never stops frothing, never stops fighting against the terrible "hard realities" of racism, political opportunism and the morally bankrupt merchants of economic expedience. Thank heavens that some of Kunio's contemporaries are still active and on the front lines of the continuing battle. People such as Roger Obata, Canadian World

War II veteran who fought for democracy in the armed forces and still battles to set the record straight on the home front. People such as Kay Shimizu, a politically astute social worker who worked throughout the '40s and is one of the people at the helm providing leadership.

There is no doubt that the NAJC has the support of Japanese-Canadian scholars and leaders across the country. But it is by no means an elitist organization. Nor, contrary to some mean-mouthed reports, is it a bunch of young radicals. The average age of the National Council, the governing body, is around 60.

There are still a great many Japanese Canadians who fled into the woods as I did, to try to hide from our ethnicity. We learned to shun one another and to view any Japanese-Canadian gathering as a gaggle of ghettoized geese. One of my points of rediscovery came when I found that I could actually have Japanese-Canadian friends. It was something like my first women's liberation meetings in the '60s when I met articulate, challenging, stimulating women - some who terrified me with their intellectual shrapnel. Where had all the kitchen talk gone?

It was a surprise to meet and like and respect my fellow geese. I crept on board the Redress ship with all ten toes still intact, intending to set sail with them to slay the dragon of racism and save democracy. A ship of friends, unlike a ship of fools, is capable of quelling storms, and unsinkable friendships are the most formidable boats in the world. What an armada we are, I thought, and what a fool I was, I soon learned. Japanese-Canadian friends, no more nor less than women friends or friends joined for any cause, are just your regular people with sensitivities and easily wounded pride. And when political wizards are at work, storms are brewing. But the ship is by no means wrecked. There continue to be many heartwarming moments.

Speaking at a meeting at Harbord Collegiate attended by more than 500 Japanese Canadians, David Suzuki referred to the National Association of Japanese Canadians as the beginnings of a national community. We are a minority among minorities, hailing one another across huge distances as we go about the business of gathering our shipmates from their rafts and logs. Today we are becoming a community that is increasingly conscious of its responsibility to the wider society, to make sure that the Japanese-Canadian story is not repeated in any other Canadian community. We are a national community in a process of political maturation. Our strategies are not written in stone. Gradually we are becoming less frightened of the rocking boat as it rides through political storms.

Although the will to destroy our small ship has been made amply evident, we have more friends today than we had in the '40s. And more than anything else, I believe it's the love that comes through our friends in the media and elsewhere that will rescue us. We are drawn to life, Rollo May says, by love. Our new courage is evidence of love. And the Ian Mackenzies who talk their "hard realities" will not destroy the "frothy idealism" that keeps our compass pointed to a better world.

For me, the beginning, middle and end of redress has been reduced to a wish for community. During the last two years, although a new national Japanese-Canadian community has been coming into being, some old community members have been badly and needlessly hurt and confused in the political machinations. Redress, for me, has already been lost and won. The cup is half-empty and half-full.

My recent experiences in the political world have disabused me of my more grandiose dreams. I used to think that a people who had been persecuted were somehow made special by it and carried with them secrets, tales of transformation, new dimensions of compassion. I dreamed that the collective Japanese-Canadian voice could startle the country with its beauty, with its stronghearted generosity, with its will to fight for the oppressed. I dreamed that the moral hunger of people could be so filled by the nobility of our vision that we would be released from our tyrannies of greed and meanness of spirit. I dreamed that an unmistakable cry of love, for one another, for Canada and for all who suffer, would transcend all our other cries.

But one person's dream is another's nightmare. This has been a time to drop my fantasies and to accept other promptings.

It's a hallmark of the oppressed that our energy turns against ourselves. The challenge that faces us all is to discover the ways in which we have been oppressors of our own. As a country, as a community and as individuals we show maturity when we assume responsibility toward those we harm. Only the most infantile can claim to be pure victim. Only the mature concern themselves with their roles as victimizers.

Japanese-Canadian redress is an occasion for senators and members of Parliament, no less than for Japanese Canadians, to discover the extent of our woundedness.

These days I do feel tired of the Japanese-Canadian focus, of the victim/victimizer question and of political warfare. The place that is without question the closest spot to home, the safest place that I can imagine, is that basement room where the three of us sit and wait - sometimes with only a candle and the grey light from the windows as our sources of light.

▼▼▼▼▼▼▼▼▼

# '*I'm Not Racist But...*'

■

## NEIL BISSOONDATH

*S*omeone recently said that racism is as Canadian as maple syrup. I have no argument with that. History provides us with ample proof. But, for proper perspective, let us remember that it is also as American as apple pie, as French as croissants, as Jamaican as ackee, as Indian as aloo, as Chinese as chow mein, as .... Well, there's an entire menu to be written. This is not by way of excusing it. Murder and rape, too, are international, multicultural, as innate to the darker side of the human experience. But we must be careful that the inevitable rage evoked does not blind us to the larger context.

The word "racism" is a discomforting one: It is so vulnerable to manipulation. We can, if we so wish, apply it to any incident involving people of different colour. And therein lies the danger. During the heat of altercation, we seize, as terms of abuse, on whatever is most obvious about the other person. It is, often, a question of unfortunate convenience. A woman, because of her sex, easily becomes a female dog

■■■■■■■■■■■■■■■■■■■■■■

Neil Bissoondath is a Canadian novelist and short-story writer. Born in Trinidad in 1955, he moved to Toronto at the age of eighteen to complete a degree in French at York University in Toronto. He has published a collection of short stories, *Digging Up The Mountains*, and a novel, *A Casual Brutality*.

or an intimate part of her anatomy. A large person might be dubbed "a stupid ox," a small person "a little" whatever. And so a black might become "a nigger," a white "a honky," an Asian "a paki," a Chinese "a chink," an Italian "a wop," a French-Canadian "a frog."

There is nothing pleasant about these terms; they assault every decent sensibility. Even so, I once met someone who, in a stunning surge of naiveté, used them as simple descriptives and not as terms of racial abuse. She was horrified to learn the truth. While this may have been an extreme case, the point is that the use of such patently abusive words may not always indicate racial or cultural distaste. They may indicate ignorance or stupidity or insensitivity, but pure racial hatred - such as the Nazis held for Jews, or the Ku Klux Klan for blacks - is a thankfully rare commodity.

Ignorance, not the willful kind but that which comes from lack of experience, is often indicated by that wonderful phrase, "I'm not racist but . . . ." I think of the mover, a friendly man, who said, "I'm not racist, but the Chinese are the worst drivers on the road." He was convinced this was so because the shape of their eyes, as far as he could surmise, denied them peripheral vision.

Or the oil company executive, an equally warm and friendly man, who, looking for an apartment in Toronto, rejected buildings with East Indian tenants not because of their race - he was telling me this, after all - but because he was given to understand that cockroaches were symbols of good luck in their culture and that, when they moved into a new home, friends came by with gift-wrapped roaches.

Neither of these men thought of himself as racist, and I believe they were not, deep down. (The oil company executive made it clear he would not hesitate to have me as a neighbour; my East Indian descent was of no consequence to him, my horror of cockroaches was.) Yet their comments, so innocently delivered, would open them to the accusation, justifiably so if this were all one knew about them. But it is a charge which would undoubtedly be wounding to them. It is difficult to recognize one's own misconceptions.

True racism is based, more often than not, on willful ignorance, and an acceptance of - and comfort with - stereotype. We like to think, in this country, that our multicultural mosaic will help nudge us into a greater openness. But multiculturalism as we know it indulges in stereotype, depends on it for a dash of colour and the flash of dance. It fails to address the most basic questions people have about each other: Do those men doing the Dragon Dance really all belong to secret criminal societies? Do those women dressed in saris really coddle cockroaches for luck? Do those people in dreadlocks all smoke marijuana and live on welfare? Such questions do not seem to be the concern of the government's multicultural programs, superficial and exhibitionistic as they have become.

So the struggle against stereotype, the basis of all racism, becomes a purely personal one. We must beware of the impressions we create. A friend of mine once commented that, from talking to West Indians, she has the impression that their one great cultural contribution to the world is in the oft-repeated boast that "We (unlike everyone else) know how to party."

There are dangers, too, in community response. We must be wary of the self-appointed activists who seem to pop up in the media at every given opportunity spouting the rhetoric of retribution, mining distress for personal, political and professional gain. We must be skeptical about those who depend on conflict for their sense of self, the non-whites who need to feel themselves victims of racism, the whites who need to feel themselves purveyors of it. And we must be sure that, in addressing the problem, we do not end up creating it. Does the *Miss Black Canada Beauty Contest* still exist? I hope not. Not only do I find beauty contests offensive, but a racially segregated one even more so. What would the public reaction be, I wonder, if every year CTV broadcast the *Miss White Canada Beauty Pageant*? We give community-service awards only to blacks: Would we be comfortable with such awards only for whites? In Quebec, there are The Association of Black Nurses, The Association of Black Artists, The Congress of Black Jurists. Play tit for tat: The Associations of White Nurses, White Artists, White Jurists: visions of apartheid. Let us be frank, racism for one is racism for others.

Finally, and perhaps most important, let us beware of abusing the word itself.

# The Man From Mars

■

## MARGARET ATWOOD

long time ago Christine was walking through the park. She was still wearing her tennis dress; she hadn't had time to shower and change, and her hair was held back with an elastic band. Her chunky reddish face, exposed with no softening fringe, looked like a Russian peasant's, but without the elastic band the hair got in her eyes. The afternoon was too hot for April; the indoor courts had been steaming, her skin felt poached.

The sun had brought the old men out from wherever they spent the winter: she had read a story recently about one who lived for three years in a manhole. They sat weedishly on the benches or lay on the grass with their heads on squares of used newspaper. As she passed, their wrinkled toadstool faces drifted toward her, drawn by the movement of her body, then floated away again, uninterested.

The squirrels were out too, foraging; two or three of them moved toward her in darts and pauses, eyes fixed on her expectantly, mouths

■ ■ ■ ■ ■ ■ ■ ■ ■ ■ ■ ■ ■ ■ ■ ■ ■ ■ ■ ■ ■ ■ ■ ■ ■ ■

Margaret Atwood was born in Ottawa in 1939. She is one of Canada's leading poets, novelists, and critics. Her works include the award-winning *Circle Game*, *Survival: A Thematic Guide To Canadian Literature*, *The Handmaid's Tale*, and *Cat's Eye*. She lives in Toronto with writer Graeme Gibson and daughter Jess.

▼▼▼▼▼▼▼▼▼

with the ratlike receding chins open to show the yellowed front teeth. Christine walked faster, she had nothing to give them. People shouldn't feed them, she thought, it makes them anxious and they get mangy.

Halfway across the park she stopped to take off her cardigan. As she bent over to pick up her tennis racquet again someone touched her on her freshly-bared arm. Christine seldom screamed; she straightened up suddenly, gripping the handle of her racquet. It was not one of the old men, however: it was a dark-haired boy of twelve or so.

"Excuse me," he said, "I search for Economics Building. It is there?" He motioned toward the west.

Christine looked at him more closely. She had been mistaken: he was not young, just short. He came a little above her shoulder, but then, she was above the average height; "statuesque," her mother called it when she was straining. He was also what was referred to in their family as "a person from another culture": Oriental without a doubt, though perhaps not Chinese. Christine judged he must be a foreign student and gave him her official welcoming smile. In high school she had been President of the United Nations Club; that year her school had been picked to represent the Egyptian delegation at the Mock Assembly. It had been an unpopular assignment - nobody wanted to be the Arabs - but she had seen it through. She had made rather a good speech about the Palestinian refugees.

"Yes," she said, "that's it over there. The c    with the flat roof. See it?"

The man had been smiling nervously a        time. He was wearing glasses with transparent plast       ich his eyes bulged up at her as though throu           had not followed where she was pointing. l.                 small pad of green paper and a ballpoint pen.

"You make map," he said.

Christine set down her tennis racquet and dre       l map. "We are here," she said, pronouncing distinctly. "You g  this way. The building is here." She indicated the route with a dotted line and an X. The man leaned close to her, watching the progress of the map attentively; he smelled of cooked cauliflower and an unfamiliar brand of hair grease. When she had finished Christine handed the paper and pen back to him with a terminal smile.

"Wait," the man said. He tore the piece of paper with the map off the pad, folded it carefully and put it in his jacket pocket; the jacket sleeves came down over his wrists and had threads at the edges. He began to write something; she noticed with a slight feeling of revulsion that the nails and the ends of his fingertips were so badly bitten they seemed almost deformed. Several of his fingers were blue from the leaky ballpoint.

"Here is my name," he said, holding the pad out to her.

Christine read an odd assemblage of G's, Y's and N's, neatly printed in block letters. "Thank you," she said.

"You now write *your* name," he said, extending the pen.

Christine hesitated. If this had been a person from her own culture she would have thought he was trying to pick her up. But then, people from her own culture never tried to pick her up: she was too big. The only one who had made the attempt was the Moroccan waiter at the beer parlour where they sometimes went after meetings, and he had been direct. He had just intercepted her on the way to the Ladies' Room and asked and she said no; that had been that. This man was not a waiter though but a student; she didn't want to offend him. In his culture, whatever it was, this exchange of names on pieces of paper was probably a formal politeness, like saying Thank You. She took the pen from him.

"That is a very pleasant name," he said. He folded the paper and placed it in his jacket pocket with the map.

Christine felt she had done her duty. "Well, goodbye," she said, "it was nice to have met you." She bent for her tennis racquet but he had already stooped and retrieved it and was holding it with both hands in front of him, like a captured banner.

"I carry this for you."

"Oh no, please. Don't bother, I am in a hurry," she said, articulating clearly. Deprived of her tennis racquet she felt weaponless. He started to saunter along the path; he was not nervous at all now, he seemed completely at ease.

"Vous parlez français?" he asked conversationally.

"Oui, un petit peu," she said. "Not very well." How am I going to get my racquet away from him without being rude? she was wondering.

"Mais vous avez un bel accent." His eyes goggled at her through the glasses: was he being flirtatious? She was well aware that her accent was wretched.

"Look," she said, for the first time letting her impatience show, "I really have to go. Give me my racquet, please."

He quickened his pace but gave no sign of returning the racquet. "Where you are going?"

"Home," she said. "My house."

"I go with you now," he said hopefully.

"*No,*" she said: she would have to be firm with him. She made a lunge and got a grip on her racquet; after a brief tug of war it came free.

"Goodbye," she said, turning away from his puzzled face and setting off at what she hoped was a discouraging jog-trot. It was like walking away from a growling dog, you shouldn't let on you were frightened. Why should she be frightened anyway? He was only half her size and she had the tennis racquet, there was nothing he could do to her.

Although she did not look back she could tell he was still following. Let there be a streetcar, she thought, and there was one, but it was far down the line, stuck behind a red light. He appeared at her side, breathing audibly, a moment after she reached the stop. She gazed ahead, rigid.

"You are my friend," he said tentatively.

Christine relented: he hadn't been trying to pick her up after all, he was a stranger, he just wanted to meet some of the local people; in his place she would have wanted the same thing.

"Yes," she said, doling him out a smile.

"That is good," he said. "My country is very far."

Christine couldn't think of an apt reply. "That's interesting," she said. "Tres interessant." The streetcar was coming at last; she opened her purse and got out a ticket.

"I go with you now," he said. His hand clamped on her arm above the elbow.

"You . . . stay . . . *here,*" Christine said, resisting the impulse to shout but pausing between each word as though for a deaf person. She detached his hand - his hold was quite feeble and could not compete with her tennis biceps - and leapt off the curb and up the streetcar steps, hearing with relief the doors grind shut behind her. Inside the car and a block away she permitted herself a glance out a side window. He was standing where she had left him; he seemed to be writing something on his little pad of paper,

When she reached home she had only time for a snack, and even then she was almost late for the Debating Society. The topic was, "Resolved: That War Is Obsolete." Her team took the affirmative, and won.


Christine came out of her last examination feeling depressed. It was not the exam that depressed her but the fact that it was the last one: it meant the end of the school year. She dropped into the coffee shop as usual, then went home early because there didn't seem to be anything else to do.

"Is that you, dear?" her mother called from the livingroom. She must have heard the front door close. Christine went in and flopped on the sofa, disturbing the neat pattern of the cushions.

"How was your exam, dear?" her mother asked.

"Fine," said Christine flatly. It had been fine, she had passed. She was not a brilliant student, she knew that, but she was conscientious. Her professors always wrote things like "A serious attempt" and "Well thought out but perhaps lacking in *élan*" on her term papers; they gave her B's, the occasional B+. She was taking Political Science and Economics, and hoped for a job with the Government after she graduated; with her father's connections she had a good chance.

"That's nice."

Christine felt, resentfully, that her mother had only a hazy idea of what an exam was. She was arranging gladioli in a vase; she had rubber gloves on to protect her hands as she always did when engaged in what she called "housework." As far as Christine could tell her housework consisted of arranging flowers in vases: daffodils and tulips and hyacinths through gladioli, iris and roses, all the way to asters and mums. Sometimes she cooked, elegantly and with chafing-dishes, but she thought of it as a hobby. The girl did everything else. Christine thought it faintly sinful to have a girl. The only ones available now were either foreign or pregnant; their expressions usually suggested they were being taken advantage of somehow. But her mother asked what they would do otherwise, they'd either have to go into a Home or stay in their own countries, and Christine had to agree this was probably true. It was hard anyway to argue with her mother, she was so delicate, so preserved-looking, a harsh breath would scratch the finish.

"An interesting young man phoned today," her mother said. She had finished the gladioli and was taking off her rubber gloves. "He asked to speak with you and when I said you weren't in we had quite a little chat. You didn't tell me about him, dear." She put on the glasses which she wore on a decorative chain around her neck, a signal that she was in her modern, intelligent mood rather than her old-fashioned whimsical one.

"Did he leave his name?" Christine asked. She knew a lot of young men but they didn't often call her, they conducted their business with her in the coffee shop or after meetings.

"He's a person from another culture. He said he would call back later."

Christine had to think a moment. She was vaguely acquainted with several people from other cultures, Britain mostly; they belonged to the Debating Society.

"He's studying Philosophy in Montreal," her mother prompted. "He sounded French."

Christine began to remember the man in the park. "I don't think he's French, exactly," she said.

Her mother had taken off her glasses again and was poking absentmindedly at a bent gladiolus. "Well, he sounded French." She meditated, flowery sceptre in hand. "I think it would be nice if you had him to tea."

Christine's mother did her best. She had two other daughters, both of whom took after her. They were beautiful, one was well married already and the other would clearly have no trouble. Her friends consoled her about Christine by saying, "She's not fat, she's just big-boned, it's the father's side," and "Christine is so healthy." Her other daughters had never gotten involved in activities when they were at school, but since Christine could not possibly ever be beautiful even if she took off weight, it was just as well she was so athletic and political, it was a good thing she had interests. Christine's mother tried to encourage her interests whenever possible. Christine could tell when she was making an extra effort, there was a reproachful edge to her voice.

She knew her mother expected enthusiasm but she could not supply it. "I don't know, I'll have to see," she said dubiously.

"You look tired, darling," said her mother. "Perhaps you'd like a glass of milk."

Christine was in the bathtub when the phone rang. She was not prone to fantasy but when she was in the bathtub she often pretended she was a dolphin, a game left over from one of the girls who used to bathe her when she was small. Her mother was being bell-voiced and gracious in the hall; then there was a tap at the door.

"It's that nice young French student, Christine," her mother said.

"Tell him I'm in the bathtub," Christine said, louder than necessary. "He isn't French."

She could hear her mother frowning. "That wouldn't be very polite, Christine. I don't think he'd understand."

"Oh all right," Christine said. She heaved herself out of the bathtub, swathed her pink bulk in a towel and splattered to the phone.

"Hello," she said gruffly. At a distance he was not pathetic, he was a nuisance. She could not imagine how he had tracked her down: most likely he went through the phone book, calling all the numbers with her last name until he hit on the right one.

"It is your friend."

"I know," she said. "How are you?"

"I am very fine." There was a long pause, during which Christine had a vicious urge to say, "Well, goodbye then," and hang up; but she was aware of her mother poised figure-like in her bedroom doorway. Then he said, "I hope you also are very fine."

"Yes," said Christine. She wasn't going to participate.

"I come to tea," he said.

This took Christine by surprise. "You do?"

"Your pleasant mother ask me. I come Thursday, four o'clock."

"Oh," Christine said, ungraciously.

"See you then," he said, with the conscious pride of one who has mastered a difficult idiom.

Christine set down the phone and went along the hall. Her mother was in her study, sitting innocently at her writing desk.

"Did you ask him to tea on Thursday?"

"Not exactly, dear," her mother said. "I did mention he might come round to tea *some*time, though."

"Well, he's coming Thursday. Four o'clock."

"What's wrong with that?" her mother said serenely. "I think it's a very nice gesture for us to make. I do think you might try to be a little more co-operative." She was pleased with herself.

"Since you invited him," said Christine, "you can bloody well stick around and help me entertain him. I don't want to be left making nice gestures all by myself."

"Christine *dear*," her mother said, above being shocked. "You ought to put on your dressing gown, you'll catch a chill."

After sulking for an hour Christine tried to think of the tea as a cross between an examination and an executive meeting: not enjoyable, certainly, but to be got through as tactfully as possible. And it was a nice gesture. When the cakes her mother had ordered arrived from *The Patisserie* on Thursday morning she began to feel slightly festive; she even resolved to put on a dress, a good one, instead of a skirt and blouse. After all, she had nothing against him, except the memory of the way he had grabbed her tennis racquet and then her arm. She suppressed a quick impossible vision of herself pursued around the livingroom, fending him off with thrown sofa cushions and vases of gladioli; nevertheless she told the girl they would have tea in the garden. It would be a treat for him, and there was more space outdoors.

She had suspected her mother would dodge the tea, would contrive to be going out just as he was arriving: that way she could size him up and then leave them alone together. She had done things like that to Christine before; the excuse this time was the Symphony Committee. Sure enough, her mother carefully mislaid her gloves and located them with a faked murmur of joy when the doorbell rang. Christine relished for weeks afterwards the image of her mother's dropped jaw and flawless recovery when he was introduced: he wasn't quite the foreign potentate her optimistic, veil-fragile mind had concocted.

He was prepared for celebration. He had slicked on so much hair cream that his head seemed to be covered with a tight black patent-leather cap, and he had cut the threads off his jacket sleeves. His orange tie was overpoweringly splendid. Christine noticed however as he shook her mother's suddenly-braced white glove that the ballpoint ink on his fingers was indelible. His face had broken out, possibly in anticipation of the delights in store for him; he had a tiny camera slung over his shoulder and was smoking an exotic-smelling cigarette.

Christine led him through the cool flowery softly-padded livingroom and out by the French doors into the garden. "You sit here," she said. "I will have the girl bring tea."

This girl was from the West Indies: Christine's parents had been enraptured with her when they were down at Christmas and had brought her back with them. Since that time she had become pregnant, but Christine's mother had not dismissed her. She said she was slightly disappointed but what could you expect, and she didn't see any real difference between a girl who was pregnant before you hired her and one who got that way afterwards. She prided herself on her tolerance; also there was a scarcity of girls. Strangely enough, the girl became progressively less easy to get along with. Either she did not share Christine's mother's view of her own generosity, or she felt she had gotten away with something and was therefore free to indulge in contempt. At first Christine had tried to treat her as an equal. "Don't call me 'Miss Christine,'" she had said with an imitation of light, comradely laughter. "What you want me to call you then?" the girl had said, scowling. They had begun to have brief, surly arguments in the kitchen, which Christine decided were like the arguments between one servant and another: her mother's attitude toward each of them was similar, they were not altogether satisfactory but they would have to do.

The cakes, glossy with icing, were set out on a plate and the teapot was standing ready; on the counter the electric kettle boiled. Christine headed for it, but the girl, till then sitting with her elbows on the kitchen table and watching her expressionlessly, made a dash and intercepted her. Christine waited until she had poured the water into the pot. Then, "I'll carry it out, Elvira," she said. She had just decided she didn't want the girl to see her visitor's orange tie; already, she knew, her position in the girl's eyes had suffered because no one had yet attempted to get *her* pregnant.

"What you think they pay me for, Miss Christine?" the girl said insolently. She swung toward the garden with the tray; Christine trailed her, feeling lumpish and awkward. The girl was at least as big as she was but she was big in a different way.

"Thank you, Elvira," Christine said when the tray was in place. The girl departed without a word, casting a disdainful backward glance at the frayed jacket sleeves, the stained fingers. Christine was now determined to be especially kind to him.

"You are very rich," he said.

"No," Christine protested, shaking her head; "we're not." She had never thought of her family as rich, it was one of her father's sayings that nobody made any money with the Government.

"Yes," he repeated, "you are very rich." He sat back in his lawn chair, gazing about him as though dazed.

Christine set his cup of tea in front of him. She wasn't in the habit of paying much attention to the house or the garden; they were nothing special, far from being the largest on the street; other people took care of them. But now she looked where he was looking, seeing it all as though from a different height: the long expanses, the border flowers blazing in the early-summer sunlight, the flagged patio and walks, the high walls and the silence.

He came back to her face, sighing a little. "My English is not good," he said, "but I improve."

"You do," Christine said, nodding encouragement.

He took sips of his tea, quickly and tenderly as though afraid of injuring the cup. "I like to stay here."

Christine passed him the cakes. He took only one, making a slight face as he ate it; but he had several more cups of tea while she finished the cakes. She managed to find out from him that he had come over on a Church fellowship - she could not decode the denomination - and was studying Philosophy or Theology, or possibly both. She was feeling well-disposed toward him: he had behaved himself, he had caused her no inconvenience.

The teapot was at last empty. He sat up straight in his chair, as though alerted by a soundless gong. "You look this way, please," he said. Christine saw that he had placed his miniature camera on the stone sundial her mother had shipped back from England two years before: he wanted to take her picture. She was flattered, and settled herself to pose, smiling evenly.

He took off his glasses and laid them beside his plate. For a moment she saw his myopic, unprotected eyes turned toward her, with something tremulous and confiding in them she wanted to close herself off from knowing about. The next instant he was crouched beside her, his arm around her waist as far as it could reach, his other hand covering her own hands which she had folded in her lap, his cheek jammed up against hers. She was too startled to move. The camera clicked.

He stood up at once and replaced his glasses, which glittered now with a sad triumph. "Thank you, Miss," he said to her. "I go now." He slung the camera back over his shoulder, keeping his hand on it as though to hold the lid on and prevent escape. "I send to my family; they will like."

He was out the gate and gone before Christine had recovered; then she laughed. She had been afraid he would attack her, she could admit it now, and he had; but not in the usual way. He had *raped, rapeo, rapere, rapui,* to *seize* and *carry off,* not herself but her celluloid image, and incidently that of the silver tea service, which glinted mockingly at her as the girl bore it away, carrying it regally, the insignia, the official jewels.

Christine spent the summer as she had for the past three years: she was the sailing instructress at an expensive all-girls camp near Algonquin Park. She had been a camper there, everything was familiar to her; she sailed almost better than she played tennis.

The second week she got a letter from him, postmarked Montreal and forwarded from her home address. It was printed in block letters on a piece of the green paper, two or three sentences. It began, "I hope you are well," then described the weather in monosyllables and ended, "I am fine." It was signed "Your friend." Each week she got another of these letters, more or less identical. In one of them a colour print was enclosed: himself, slightly cross-eyed and grinning hilariously, even more spindly than she remembered him against her billowing draperies, flowers exploding around them like firecrackers, one of his hands an equivocal blur in her lap, the other out of sight; on her own face, astonishment and outrage, as though he was sticking her in the behind with his hidden thumb.

She answered the first letter, but after that the seniors were in training for the races. At the end of the summer, packing to go home, she threw all the letters away.

When she had been back for several weeks she received another of the green letters. This time there was a return address printed at the top which Christine noted with foreboding was in her own city. Every day she waited for the phone to ring; she was so certain his first attempt at contact would be a disembodied voice that when he came upon her abruptly in mid-campus she was unprepared.

"How are you?"

His smile was the same, but everything else about him had deteriorated. He was, if possible, thinner; his jacket sleeves had sprouted a lush new crop of threads, as though to conceal hands now so badly bitten they appeared to have been gnawed by rodents. His hair fell over his eyes, uncut, ungreased; his eyes in the hollowed face, a delicate triangle of skin stretched on bone, jumped behind his glasses like hooked fish. He had the end of a cigarette in the corner of his mouth and as they walked he lit a new one from it.

"I'm fine," Christine said. She was thinking, I'm not going to get involved again, enough is enough, I've done my bit for internationalism. "How are you?"

"I live here now," he said. "Maybe I study Economics."

"That's nice." He didn't sound as though he was enrolled anywhere.

"I come to see you."

Christine didn't know whether he meant he had left Montreal in order to be near her or just wanted to visit her at her house as he had done in the spring; either way she refused to be implicated. They were outside the Political Science building. "I have a class here," she said. "Goodbye." She was being callous, she realized that, but a quick chop was more merciful in the long run, that was what her beautiful sisters used to say.

Afterwards she decided it had been stupid of her to let him find out where her class was. Though a timetable was posted in each of the colleges: all he had to do was look her up and record her every probable movement in block letters on his green notepad. After that day he never left her alone.

Initially he waited outside the lecture rooms for her to come out. She said Hello to him curtly at first and kept on going, but this didn't work; he followed her at a distance, smiling his changeless smile. Then she stopped speaking altogether and pretended to ignore him, but it made no difference, he followed her anyway. The fact that she was in some way afraid of him - or was it just embarrassment? - seemed only to encourage him. Her friends started to notice, asking her who he was and why he was tagging along behind her; she could hardly answer because she hardly knew.

As the weekdays passed and he showed no signs of letting up, she began to jog-trot between classes, finally to run. He was tireless, and had an amazing wind for one who smoked so heavily: he would speed along behind her, keeping the distance between them the same, as though he was a pull-toy attached to her by a string. She was aware of the ridiculous spectacle they must make, galloping across campus, something out of a cartoon short, a lumbering elephant stampeded by a smiling, emaciated mouse, both of them locked in the classic pattern of comic pursuit and flight; but she found that to race made her less nervous than to walk sedately, the skin on the back of her neck crawling with the feel of his eyes on it. At least she could use her muscles. She worked out routines, escapes: she would dash in the front door of the Ladies' Room in the coffee shop and out the back door, and he would lose the trail, until he discovered the other entrance. She would try to shake him by detours through baffling archways and corridors, but he seemed as familiar with the architectural mazes as she was herself. As a last refuge she could head for the women's dormitory and watch from safety as he was skidded to a halt by the receptionist's austere voice: men were not allowed past the entrance.

Lunch became difficult. She would be sitting, usually with other members of the Debating Society, just digging nicely into a sandwich, when he would appear suddenly as though he'd come up through an unseen manhole. She then had the choice of barging out through the crowded cafeteria, sandwich half-eaten, or finishing her lunch with him standing behind her chair, everyone at the table acutely aware of him, the conversation stilting and dwindling. Her friends learned to spot him from a distance; they posted lookouts. "Here he comes," they would whisper, helping her collect her belongings for the sprint they knew would follow.

Several times she got tired of running and turned to confront him. "What do you want?" she would ask, glowering belligerently down at him, almost clenching her fists; she felt like shaking him, hitting him.

"I wish to talk with you."

"Well, here I am," she would say. "What do you want to talk about?"

But he would say nothing; he would stand in front of her, shifting his feet, smiling perhaps apologetically (though she could never pinpoint the exact tone of that smile, chewed lips stretched apart over the nicotine-yellowed teeth, rising at the corners, flesh held stiffly in place for an invisible photographer), his eyes jerking from one part of her face to another as though he saw her in fragments.

Annoying and tedious though it was, his pursuit of her had an odd result: mysterious in itself, it rendered her equally mysterious. No one had ever found Christine mysterious before. To her parents she was a beefy heavyweight, a plodder, lacking in flair, ordinary as bread. To her sisters she was the plain one, treated with an indulgence they did not give to each other: they did not fear her as a rival. To her male friends she was the one who could be relied on. She was helpful and a hard worker, always good for a game of tennis with the athletes among them. They invited her along to drink beer with them so they could get into the cleaner, more desirable Ladies and Escorts side of the beer parlour, taking it for granted she would buy her share of the rounds. In moments of stress they confided to her their problems with women. There was nothing devious about her and nothing interesting.

Christine had always agreed with these estimates of herself. In childhood she had identified with the False Bride or the ugly sister; whenever a story had begun, "Once there was a maiden as beautiful as she was good," she had known it wasn't her. That was just how it was, but it wasn't so bad. Her parents never expected her to be a brilliant social success and weren't overly disappointed when she wasn't. She was spared the manoeuvring and anxiety she witnessed among others her age, and she even had a kind of special position among men: she was an exception, she fitted none of the categories they commonly used when talking about girls, she wasn't a tease, a cold fish, an easy lay or a snarky bitch; she was an honorary person. She had grown to share their contempt for most women.

Now however there was something about her that could not be explained. A man was chasing her, a peculiar sort of man, granted, but still a man, and he was without doubt attracted to her, he couldn't leave her alone. Other men examined her more closely than they ever had, appraising her, trying to find out what it was those twitching bespectacled eyes saw in her. They started to ask her out, though they returned from these excursions with their curiosity unsatisfied, the secret of her charm still intact. Her opaque dumpling face, her solid bear-shaped body became for them parts of a riddle no one could solve. Christine knew this and began to use it. In the bathtub she no longer imagined she was a dolphin; instead she imagined she was an elusive water-nixie, or sometimes, in moments of audacity, Marilyn Monroe. The daily chase was becoming a habit; she even looked forward to it. In addition to its other benefits she was losing weight.

All those weeks he had never phoned her or turned up at the house. He must have decided however that his tactics were not having the desired result, or perhaps he sensed she was becoming bored. The phone began to ring in the early morning or late at night when he could be sure she would be there. Sometimes he would simply breathe (she could recognize, or thought she could, the quality of his breathing), in which case she would hang up. Occasionally he would say again that he wanted to talk to her, but even when she gave him lots of time nothing else would follow. Then he extended his range: she would see him on her streetcar, smiling at her silently from a seat never closer than three away; she could feel him tracking her down her own street, though when she would break her resolve to pay no attention and would glance back he would be invisible or in the act of hiding behind a tree or hedge.

Among crowds of people and in daylight she had not really been afraid of him; she was stronger than he was and he had made no recent attempt to touch her. But the days were growing shorter and colder, it was almost November, often she was arriving home in twilight or a darkness broken only by the feeble orange streetlamps. She brooded over the possibility of razors, knives, guns; by acquiring a weapon he could quickly turn the odds against her. She avoided wearing scarves, remembering the newspaper stories about girls who had been strangled by them. Putting on her nylons in the morning gave her a funny feeling. Her body seemed to have diminished, to have become smaller than his.

Was he deranged, was he a sex maniac? He seemed so harmless, yet it was that kind who often went berserk in the end. She pictured those ragged fingers at her throat, tearing at her clothes, though she could not think of herself as screaming. Parked cars, the shrubberies near her house, the driveways on either side of it, changed as she passed them from unnoticed background to sinisterly-shadowed foreground, every detail distinct and harsh: they were places a man might crouch, leap out from. Yet every time she saw him in the clear light of morning or afternoon (for he still continued his old methods of pursuit), his aging jacket and jittery eyes convinced her that it was she herself who was the tormentor, the persecuter. She was in some sense responsible; from the folds and crevices of the body she had treated for so long as a reliable machine was emanating, against her will, some potent invisible odour, like a dog's in heat or a female moth's, that made him unable to stop following her.

Her mother, who had been too preoccupied with the unavoidable fall entertaining to pay much attention to the number of phone calls Christine was getting or to the hired girl's complaints of a man who hung up without speaking, announced that she was flying down to New York for the weekend; her father decided to go too. Christine panicked: she saw herself in the bathtub with her throat slit, the blood drooling out of her neck and running in a little spiral down the drain (for by this time she believed he could walk through walls, could be everywhere at once). The girl would do nothing to help; she might even stand in the bathroom door with her arms folded, watching. Christine arranged to spend the weekend at her married sister's.

When she arrived back Sunday evening she found the girl close to hysterics. She said that on Saturday she had gone to pull the curtains across the French doors at dusk and had found a strangely contorted face, a man's face, pressed against the glass, staring in at her from the garden. She claimed she had fainted and had almost had her baby a month too early right there on the livingroom carpet. Then she had called the police. He was gone by the time they got there but she had recognized him from the afternoon of the tea; she had informed them he was a friend of Christine's.

They called Monday evening to investigate, two of them; they were very polite, they knew who Christine's father was. Her father greeted them heartily; her mother hovered in the background, fidgeting with her porcelain hands, letting them see how frail and worried she was. She didn't like having them in the livingroom but they were necessary.

Christine had to admit he'd been following her around. She was relieved he'd been discovered, relieved also that she hadn't been the one to tell, though if he'd been a citizen of the country she would have called the police a long time ago. She insisted he was not dangerous, he had never hurt her.

"That kind don't hurt you," one of the policemen said. "They just kill you. You're lucky you aren't dead."

"Nut cases," the other one said.

Her mother volunteered that the thing about people from another culture was that you could never tell whether they were insane or not because their ways were so different. The policeman agreed with her, deferential but also condescending, as though she was a royal halfwit who had to be humoured.

"You know where he lives?" the first policeman asked. Christine had long ago torn up the letter with his address on it; she shook her head.

"We'll have to pick him up tomorrow then," he said. "Think you can keep him talking outside your class if he's waiting for you?"

After questioning her they held a murmured conversation with her father in the front hall. The girl, clearing away the coffee cups, said if they didn't lock him up she was leaving, she wasn't going to be scared half out of her skin like that again.

Next day when Christine came out of her Modern History lecture he was there, right on schedule. He seemed puzzled when she did not begin to run. She approached him, her heart thumping with treachery and the prospect of freedom. Her body was back to its usual size; she felt herself a giantess, self-controlled, invulnerable.

"How are you?" she asked, smiling brightly.

He looked at her with distrust.

"How have you been?" she ventured again. His own perennial smile faded; he took a step back from her.

"This the one?" said the policeman, popping out from behind a notice board like a Keystone Cop and laying a competent hand on the worn jacket shoulder. The other policeman lounged in the background; force would not be required.

"Don't *do* anything to him," she pleaded as they took him away. They nodded and grinned, respectful, scornful. He seemed to know perfectly well who they were and what they wanted.

The first policeman phoned that evening to make his report. Her father talked with him, jovial and managing. She herself was now out of the picture; she had been protected, her function was over.

"What did they *do* to him?" she asked anxiously as he came back into the livingroom. She was not sure what went on in police stations.

"They didn't do anything to him," he said, amused by her concern. "They could have booked him for Watching and Besetting, they wanted to know if I'd like to proffer charges. But it's not worth a court case: he's got a visa that says he's only allowed in the country as long as he studies in Montreal, so I told them to just ship him up there. If he turns up here again they'll deport him. They went around to his rooming house, his rent's two weeks overdue; the landlady said she was on the point of kicking him out. He seems happy enough to be getting his back rent paid and a free train ticket to Montreal." He paused. "They couldn't get anything out of him though."

"*Out* of him?" Christine asked.

"They tried to find out why he was doing it; following you, I mean." Her father's eyes swept her as though it was a riddle to him also. "They said when they asked him about that he just clammed up. Pretended he didn't understand English. He understood well enough, but he wasn't answering."

Christine thought this was the end, but somehow between his arrest and the departure of the train he managed to elude his escort long enough for one more phone call.

"I see you again," he said. He didn't wait for her to hang up.

Now that he was no longer an embarrassing present reality he could be talked about, he could become an amusing story. In fact he was the only amusing story Christine had to tell, and telling it preserved both for herself and for others the aura of her strange allure. Her friends and the men who continued to ask her out speculated about his motives. One suggested he had wanted to marry her so he could remain in the country; another said that oriental men were fond of well-built women: "It's your Rubens quality."

Christine thought about him a lot. She had not been attracted to him, rather the reverse, but as an idea only he was a romantic figure, the one man who had found her irresistible; though she often wondered, inspecting her unchanged pink face and hefty body in her full-length mirror, just what it was about her that had done it. She avoided whenever it was proposed the theory of his insanity: it was only that there was more than one way of being sane.

But a new acquaintance, hearing the story for the first time, had a different explanation. "So he got you too," he said, laughing. "That has to be the same guy who was hanging around our day camp a year ago this summer. He followed all the girls like that. A short guy, Japanese or something, glasses, smiling all the time."

"Maybe it was another one," Christine said.

"There couldn't be two of them, everything fits. This was a pretty weird guy."

"What . . . *kind* of girls did he follow?" Christine asked.

"Oh, just anyone who happened to be around. But if they paid any attention to him at first, if they were nice to him or anything, he was unshakeable. He was a bit of a pest, but harmless."

Christine ceased to tell her amusing story. She had been one among many, then. She went back to playing tennis, she had been neglecting her game.

A few months later the policeman who had been in charge of the case telephoned her again.

"Like you to know, Miss, that fellow you were having the trouble with was sent back to his own country. Deported."

"What for?" Christine asked. "Did he try to come back here?"

Maybe she had been special after all, maybe he had dared everything for her.

"Nothing like it," the policeman said. "He was up to the same tricks in Montreal but he really picked the wrong woman this time - a Mother Superior of a convent. They don't stand for things like that in Quebec - had him out of here before he knew what happened. I guess he'll be better off in his own place."

"How old was she?" Christine asked, after a silence.

"Oh, around sixty, I guess."

"Thank you very much for letting me know," Christine said in her best official manner. "It's such a relief." She wondered if the policeman had called to make fun of her.

She was almost crying when she put down the phone. What *had* he wanted from her then? A Mother Superior. Did she really look sixty, did she look like a mother? What did convents mean? Comfort, charity? Refuge? Was it that something had happened to him, some intolerable strain just from being in this country; her tennis dress and exposed legs too much for him, flesh and money seemingly available everywhere but withheld from him wherever he turned, the nun the symbol of some final distortion, the robe and the veil reminiscent to his nearsighted eyes of the women of his homeland, the ones he was able to understand? But he was back in his own country, remote from her as another planet; she would never know.

He hadn't forgotten her though. In the spring she got a postcard with a foreign stamp and the familiar block-letter writing. On the front was a picture of a temple. He was fine, he hoped she was fine also, he was her friend. A month later another print of the picture he had taken in the garden arrived, in a sealed manila envelope otherwise empty.

Christine's aura of mystery soon faded; anyway, she herself no longer believed in it. Life became again what she had always expected. She graduated with mediocre grades and went into the Department of Health and Welfare; she did a good job, and was seldom discriminated against for being a woman because nobody thought of her as one. She could afford a pleasant-sized apartment, though she did not put much energy into decorating it. She played less and less tennis; what had been muscle with a light coating of fat turned gradually to fat with a thin substratum of muscle. She began to get headaches.

As the years were used up and the war began to fill the newspapers and magazines, she realized which eastern country he had actually been from. She had known the name but it hadn't registered at the time, it was such a minor place; she could never keep them separate in her mind.

But though she tried, she couldn't remember the name of the city, and the postcard was long gone - had he been from the North or the South, was he near the battle zone or safely far from it? Obsessively she bought the magazines and poured over the available photographs, dead villagers, soldiers on the march, colour blowups of frightened or angry faces, spies being executed; she studied maps, she watched the late-night newscasts, the distant country and terrain becoming almost more familiar to her than her own. Once or twice she thought she could recognize him but it was no use, they all looked like him.

Finally she had to stop looking at the pictures. It bothered her too much, it was bad for her; she was beginning to have nightmares in which he was coming through the French doors of her mother's house in his shabby jacket, carrying a packsack and a rifle and a huge bouquet of richly-coloured flowers. He was smiling in the same way but with blood streaked over his face, partly blotting out the features. She gave her television set away and took to reading nineteenth-century novels instead; Trollope and Galsworthy were her favourites. When, despite herself, she would think about him, she would tell herself that he had been crafty and agile-minded enough to survive, more or less, in her country, so surely he would be able to do it in his own, where he knew the language. She could not see him in the army, on either side; he wasn't the type, and to her knowledge he had not believed in any particular ideology. He would be something nondescript, something in the background, like herself; perhaps he had become an interpreter.

▼▼▼▼▼▼▼▼▼

# *T*he Nun Who Returned to Ireland

■

## R O C H    C A R R I E R

fter my first day of school I ran back to the house, holding out my reader.

"Mama, I learned how to read!" I announced.

"This is an important day," she replied; "I want your  father to be here to see."

We waited for him.  I waited as I'd never waited before.  And as soon as his step rang out on the floor of the gallery, my first reader was open on my knees and my finger was pointing to the first letter in a short sentence.

"Your son learned to read today," my mother declared through the screen door.  She was as excited as I.

"Well, well!" said my father.  "Things happen fast nowadays.  Pretty soon, son, you'll be able to do like me - read the newspaper upside down in your sleep!"

"Listen to me!" I said.

And I read the sentence I'd learned in school that day, from Sister

■ ■ ■ ■ ■ ■ ■ ■ ■ ■ ■ ■ ■ ■ ■ ■ ■ ■ ■ ■ ■

Roch Carrier was born in Sainte-Justine-de-Dorchester, a small village in Quebec, in 1937, and studied in Montreal and at Le Sorbonne in Paris.  He has written plays, short stories,  novels, poems, and a series of lectures on Quebec literature.  He is one of the most widely read Quebecois authors in English Canada as well as in Quebec.

Brigitte. But instead of picking me up and lifting me in his arms, my father looked at my mother and my mother didn't come and kiss her little boy who'd learned to read so quickly.

"What's going on here?" my father asked.

"I'd say it sounds like English," said my mother. "Show me your book." (She read the sentence I'd learned to decipher.) "I'd say you're reading as if you were English. Start again."

I reread the short sentence.

"You're reading with an English accent!" my mother exclaimed.

"I'm reading the way Sister Brigitte taught me."

"Don't tell me he's learning his own mother tongue in English," my father protested.

I had noticed that Sister Brigitte didn't speak the way we did, but that was quite natural because we all knew that nuns don't do anything the way other people do: they didn't dress like everybody else, they didn't get married, they didn't have children and they always lived in hiding. But as far as knowing whether Sister Brigitte had an English accent, how could I? I'd never heard a single word of English.

Over the next few days I learned that she hadn't been born in our village; it seemed very strange that someone could live in the village without being born there, because everyone else in the village had been born in the village.

Our parents weren't very pleased that their children were learning to read their mother tongue with an English accent. In whispers, they started to say that Sister Brigitte was Irish - that she hadn't even been born in Canada. Monsieur Cassidy, the undertaker, was Irish too, but he'd been born in the village, while Sister Brigitte had come from Ireland.

"Where's Ireland?" I asked my mother.

"It's a very small, very green little country in the ocean, far, far away."

As our reading lessons proceeded I took pains to pronounce the vowels as Sister Brigitte did, to emphasize the same syllables as she; I was so impatient to read the books my uncles brought back from their far-off colleges. Suddenly it was important for me to know.

"Sister Brigitte, where's Ireland?"

She put down her book.

"Ireland is the country where my parents were born, and my grandparents and my great-grandparents. And I was born in Ireland too. I was a little girl in Ireland. When I was a child like you I lived in Ireland. We had horses and sheep. Then the Lord asked me to become his servant . . . ."

"What does that mean?"

"The Lord asked me if I wanted to become a nun. I said yes. So then I left my family and I forgot Ireland and my village."

"Forgot your village?"

I could see in her eyes that she didn't want to answer my question.

"Ever since, I've been teaching young children. Some of the children who were your age when I taught them are grandparents now, old grandparents."

Sister Brigitte's face, surrounded by her starched coif, had no age; I learned that she was old, very old, because she had been a teacher to grandparents.

"Have you ever gone back to Ireland?"

"God didn't want to send me back."

"You must miss your country."

"God asked me to teach little children to read and write so every child could read the great book of life."

"Sister Brigitte, you're older than our grandparents! Will you go back to Ireland before you die?"

The old nun must have known from my expression that death was so remote for me I could speak of it quite innocently, as I would speak of the grass or the sky. She said simply:

"Let's go on with our reading. School children in Ireland aren't so disorderly as you."

All that autumn we applied ourselves to our reading; by December we could read the brief texts Sister Brigitte wrote on the blackboard herself, in a pious script we tried awkwardly to imitate; in every text the word Ireland always appeared. It was by writing the word Ireland that I learned to form a capital I.

After Christmas holidays Sister Brigitte wasn't at the classroom door to greet us; she was sick. From our parents' whispers we learned that Sister Brigitte had lost her memory. We weren't surprised. We knew that old people always lose their memories and Sister Brigitte was an old person because she had been a teacher to grandparents.

Late in January, the nuns in the convent discovered that Sister Brigitte had left her room. They looked everywhere for her, in all the rooms and all the classrooms. Outside, a storm was blowing gusts of snow and wind; you couldn't see Heaven or earth, as they said. Sister Brigitte, who had spent the last few weeks in her bed, had fled into the storm. Some men from the village spotted her black form in the blizzard; beneath her vast mantle she was barefoot. When the men asked her where she was going, Sister Brigitte replied in English that she was going home, to Ireland.

▼▼▼▼▼▼▼▼▼

# Building All Over Again

*Advice to the Young*

*I'm Just Me: Adrienne Clarkson*

*Black Like Me*

*Rebirth*

*A Boat Girl Grows Up*

*The Management of Grief*

# *Advice To The Young*

■

## M I R I A M   W A D D I N G T O N

1 Keep bees and
grow asparagus,
watch the tides
and listen to the
wind instead of
the politicians
make up your own
stories and believe
them if you want to
live the good life.

2 All rituals
are instincts
never fully
trust them but
study to im-
prove biology
with reason.

3 Digging trenches
for asparagus
is good for the
muscles and
waiting for the
plants to settle
teaches patience
to those who are
usually in too
much of a hurry.

4 There is morality
in bee-keeping
it teaches how
not to be afraid
of the bee swarm
it teaches how
not to be afraid of
finding new places
and building in them
all over again.

# *I'm Just Me:*

## *An Interview with Adrienne Clarkson*

■

# M A G G I E      G O H

*A*drienne Clarkson was born in 1939 in Hong Kong. At the age of three, she fled to Canada with her parents, William and Ethel Poy, and her brother, Neville, when the Japanese invaded Hong Kong. Clarkson grew up in Ottawa and achieved remarkable success in various careers as university lecturer, TV host and producer, Agent-general for Ontario in France, and publisher.

MG: *I understand that you were only three when your family moved to Canada. Do you have any memories at all of your early years in Hong Kong and the journey to Canada?*

AC: Well, I have only scattered memories of Hong Kong then. Little pieces of landscape remain in my mind. When I went back to Hong Kong in my adolescence, my ideas mingled and I found myself asking, "Did I see this then? . . . Did I just see it?" We left Hong Kong during the war, which was only a twelve-day war

■ ■ ■ ■ ■ ■ ■ ■ ■ ■ ■ ■ ■ ■ ■ ■ ■ ■ ■ ■ ■

Maggie Goh was born in Malaysia and grew up in Singapore, where she had "a very British education" and began her career in publishing. She moved to Canada with her husband and two sons in 1977. "We have grown roots. We have a Canadian-born daughter and I no longer loathe winter."

91

because the Japanese overran Hong Kong. I don't remember any of that, but I do remember a little of the journey over. We were refugees, and I have memories of the big boat that we came over on.

MG:   *How do you think your parents adapted to Canada? Did they have any problems adjusting to a new country with two young children?*

AC:   It's difficult of course, when you're thrown out of your country because of war and you come to another country without anything, just one suitcase apiece. But my parents are both very strong, tough-minded people and that always helps. Also, my father had been born in Australia and only returned to his village in China and then to Hong Kong when he was 19, so he spoke English well, which helped, and he liked Canada immediately because the wide-open spaces reminded him of Australia. He was very athletic, and here he could have his sports again - he took to skiing right away, for instance -so he loved it all. However, I think it was harder for my mother because she'd never been in a kitchen before, she had always had servants, and here she was at 28 with two little children in a small house in Ottawa not even knowing how to cook. Fortunately, there were people who were kind to us, and a very nice woman called Alice Crew who was a distant relative of a Canadian we had known in Hong Kong, taught her how to cook. I think my mother always resented it in a way, but on the other hand, she never made us aware of it. I was brought up with not very much regret or feeling of regret. Whatever the circumstances, my parents never ever said, "Oh, if only things had been different." My father's not that kind of person. We were always taught to take tomorrow as the next day. I think my mother would have tended more to be regretful, but she basically didn't like to be defeated by anything, so she didn't show it to us. I was brought up by very strong people.

MG:   *So you never had the feeling that your parents were torn? They made up their minds that Canada was now home and that was that?*

AC:     Right. I was never brought up with the feeling that what we had left behind was better than what we had, and in a way my parents almost over-compensated by saying, "Look at this marvellous country, look at these wonderful schools, look at this beautiful landscape." As children, we took to it right away. We didn't have any money, but we had a good time. We used to borrow a car from someone from my father's village in China, a really nice old man. He had a small store in Ottawa. I think he was a sort of herbalist. Every summer he used to lend us his car for a week and we would drive all over Ontario. We went to see Niagara Falls, and we went all over the place. We really enjoyed those little trips. When we did gather up a little bit of money we bought a cottage, because my parents loved to fish. That aspect of Canadian life - fishing and living in a cottage - suited my mother's character because she was a very solitary soul and she liked gardening and all that sort of thing. It also suited my father because he was athletic and loved the outdoors. So between the two of them, we had this very healthy up-bringing, I think, where we seemed to have the best of both cultures. I've been thinking a lot about it myself as I've been writing a book about this, and I think we really did have the best of both worlds because my parents learned all the things they wanted to learn out of Canadian life and they made us learn it. Also, because my parents didn't speak a lot of Chinese at home, we learned English quickly. My father didn't learn Chinese until he went at the age of nineteen or twenty back to his village first of all and then to Hong Kong. He was brought up in a very small village in Australia where there were not many other Chinese and they didn't speak Chinese. So he basically didn't speak it that much. He learned it later though, and now he speaks it a little more. It's funny, as he grows older - he's eighty-two now - he speaks more Chinese. My mother died a year and a half ago, but while she was alive, they used to speak a reasonable amount of Chinese. But my father made a big point to us all that we must learn excellent English, do public speaking and present ourselves well. He always stressed the importance of that.

MG:  *What about your mother - Did she speak Chinese?*

AC:  Yes she did. She had a classical Chinese education as well as an English education. She went to a very good school in Hong Kong, but she left school after her senior matriculation to get married. Her longings were not intellectual. She was a very smart woman, but her longings were basically artistic and she liked painting and flowers and sewing and embroidery and all of that. In many ways, I think she was rather a frustrated artist. She always spoke Chinese with my father, and subsequently her sisters who immigrated to Canada, and with my sister-in-law, my brother's wife, who is also our second cousin from Hong Kong.

MG:  *So Chinese was spoken at home, but your parents never attempted to make you learn the language?*

AC:  No, I mean they offered it. They said, "Would you like to go to a Chinese school?" But I wasn't into that, basically. And people say, "Don't you regret it?" But I don't have regrets about it. You can't do everything in your life. I like being Chinese. I particularly enjoy the food and the health aspects of Chinese life. The older I get, the more I realize it was a great foundation for my life. But as a child, I liked Canadian life, I felt part of Canada, I went to public schools, I took part in everything, and it suited me. My interests were basically English and History - I used to go to the public library and read books about English History and French History - I was always interested in that. And I wanted to learn French right from a very early age. My brother is more Chinese, but then of course he was eight when we came and I was three, and I think that makes a lot of difference.

MG:  *Well, not knowing the language doesn't make you any less of a Chinese.*

AC:  No, not at all. I felt when I was in China, too, that it wasn't a loss because the Chinese look at overseas Chinese as part of them even if they don't speak any Chinese, and even if they're not full-bloodedly Chinese. As one of the Chinese people that took us around northern China said to me, "If you have one drop of

Chinese blood, you're Chinese to us." And it's so true. It's so different from the way people in the West look at things; they're excluding all the time, whereas the Chinese are englobing all the time.

MG:  *Amy Tan, the author of* The Joy Luck Club, *grew up in San Francisco. She said that when she visited China and stepped on Chinese soil, she felt totally Chinese. Did you have any special feelings when you returned to Hong Kong?*

AC:  Well, Hong Kong and China to me are two totally different things. I think of Hong Kong as a very British kind of place with Chinese inhabitants, and I don't think really it's China. I felt very different kinds of things when I went to China. I felt China was quite extraordinary, and I particularly enjoyed going back to my father's village in Toi San. I liked that very much. But I don't have any particular feelings for Hong Kong. If I never saw it again it would not bother me. I understand why my parents liked it *then*, I mean, they had a lovely time in the '20s and '30s. It was a very small place, less than 500 000 people, the beaches were beautiful, my father rode, they had a very elegant and interesting life. But I don't think life in Hong Kong today is anything to be admired. It has absolutely no appeal for me.

MG:  *You said earlier that instead of learning Chinese, you were much more interested in learning French. That was rather unusual in those days, wasn't it?*

AC:  Yes, I think it was. When we arrived in Canada, we lived first in a French-Canadian neighbourhood in Ottawa. My instinct always in a strange situation is to learn all about the situation and plunge right into it, not to withdraw. That's what I have in my character. So I wanted to learn French right from a very early age.

MG:  *I've read in many articles that your father was a strong influence in your life. Can you comment on this?*

AC:  Yes, he was a strong influence, not in the way that most people think of a father's influence - that they're heavy and they're dominating - he really is a very frivolous man. He's not very interested in any intellectual things at all, but he's a tremendously nice person, very charming, very elegant, a very good dancer, and lovely to be around. He's fun, he's got a great sense of humour, he likes to be around people. He was very demanding in the sense that he brought us up to be very well-mannered, to speak properly, and to always present ourselves well. However, he wasn't dominating or anything, and he never got upset. My parents were very sophisticated in their attitudes, I suppose. People have asked me, "Were they upset when you started to go out with Canadian boys who weren't Chinese?" Well, who else was there to go out with? My parents didn't want me to sit at home. My mother sewed and she wanted to make me party dresses. So I always went out with "Canadian" boys. Once I asked my father, "Dad, did it ever bother you?" He said, "Why should it? It was perfectly natural, you were brought up here. Who else were you going to see?" I was very fortunate in that I had no pressures. I went to school with other ethnic girls whose families were so heavy on them and wouldn't let them go out with anybody who wasn't from their group. I never had to deal with those sort of things.

MG: *I can see that your parents' enlightened attitudes must have helped you settle into Canada without too many problems, but did you, in all the time you were growing up, ever feel different?*

AC: I've always felt different. I still feel different. But I think it gives me my great strength. Being an outsider gives you a feeling of distance. You always know you're not part of a group, and therefore you can think on your own and you can make up your mind on your own. I always knew I was different, but then again I was very fortunate in the sense that my father's a very handsome man, my mother was an extremely beautiful woman, and so we felt, really, very attractive. And that was a big help to us, I think.

MG: *Well, so much of what a person is comes from what your parents instill into you, and I can see they always made you feel good about being yourself.*

AC: Yes. I mean, whatever problems they might have had, the feeling my parents gave us, as children and as people, was that we were really very special, very attractive. I wore glasses, but nobody made a big thing of that. My mother wore glasses, and she'd tell me when to take them off, that sort of female vanity thing. And I was very conscious of the fact that they did things for me, that we didn't have very much money and yet they were saving it for me to go to university, that the clothes that I wore my mother planned with care and bought patterns for. Everything was very centred around me and around my brother.

MG: *I suppose, coming to Canada at three, you were never burdened with that feeling of rootlessness that most older immigrants experience?*

AC: No, I don't think so. We embraced Canadian life but we also spent a lot of time with Chinese people. We would always go and eat Chinese food at the restaurant run by someone from our village. My father comes from peasant stock - from a village - and even though we gradually had more money and everything, we never lost touch with our Chinese friends. One of our good friends who used to come over and spend Sunday afternoon with us regularly was a waiter at the restaurant. He was a village friend of my father's, and he had been a houseman for a very rich woman in Ottawa. And we always had that kind of connection. We were not cut off in any way. But there weren't many people there that we shared that much with. The original Chinese who were in Ottawa at that point were people who had been in Canada for some time and had never been in Hong Kong. We were Hong Kong people, and that made us very different. And my mother, I think, felt that difference more than anyone else.

MG: *Do you ever think to yourself, "Am I Chinese, or am I Canadian?" Does that ever cross your mind?*

AC: No, it never ever occurs to me. It never, never crosses my mind, "Am I Chinese or am I Canadian?" I'm just me.

MG: *Is being Chinese important to you? Is there any value in it?*
AC: I think so. I think it made me special, I think it made me different. If I hadn't had those layers of complexity behind me which the Chinese part of me represents, I wouldn't be what I am, I wouldn't represent what I am. I think it is important to me more and more for what I do. It's important in my understanding of things. I think and I feel differently. I am, you know, the sum of enormous numbers and generations of genes obviously, so that's part of it. And then on top of it, I had the opportunity of all this Europeanized life with Canada and Europe, and I think it's made me a very layered kind of person.

MG: *Your co-host on the Fifth Estate, Eric Malling, once said that being a Chinese and a woman made you memorable. Do you agree?*
AC: Yes, I think that's true. I think being Chinese has been a definite advantage to me. I haven't been that conscious of it, but I think that's right. Certainly I was never forgotten when I was in school. That has its advantages and disadvantages. In those days, I was the only Chinese child in my year going through public school; although there were a few more in high school. And on top of that, there was the war going on and people were very sympathetic to us because we had lost our home and we'd come to Canada as refugees.

MG: *Well, on the other side of the coin, throughout your highly successful career, has being Chinese ever proved a stumbling block at all?*
AC: No, it has never, never, never been a stumbling block. In fact, I always think it's been a plus to me. Nobody has ever said to me, "This happened to you or didn't happen to you because you're Chinese." Nor have I ever felt that, and I think I would be sensitive to that. But I haven't ever experienced anything negative.

MG: *What about being a woman? Has it ever been a stumbling block?*

AC: Oh yes, most definitely so. I always felt the prejudices against women. I really resented it at university when the very intelligent men who got first class honours were invited to something called the History Club at the University of Toronto - which thank God exists no more - but women weren't. Women weren't allowed into Hart House or into the Olympic-sized swimming pool. We were not even allowed in to hear the debate between John F Kennedy and William Buckley in 1959, and we had to demonstrate. So, being a *woman* was a big stumbling block, being Chinese wasn't the one.

MG: *Even past university and out in the work world you felt the barriers?*

AC: Yes, there have always been invisible barriers there to women, and so I've been determined all my life that those barriers will go. I don't think there are barriers to people racially. I think that will go. I mean, there'll be bigotry and stuff because people want to exclude all the time, and they hate anybody who isn't one of them, but that's a small minority of people. But the female and male thing is really something you have to keep pushing at all the time. Well, look at what's still happening today.

MG: *Today I see many new immigrants who don't make an attempt to assimilate, who insist on living the way they did in their country of origin. What do you think of that?*

AC: I think that's tragic. That's really tragic - tragic for them because this is another world, and Canada has the right to expect people to be Canadians. Newcomers must learn what the situation is here, and they must learn what the rules are, and they must learn what the structure is so that they can be part of it and get the most out of it. You won't get the most out of a situation unless you're part of it, and unless you help to create the structure and plunge into it.

MG: *How do you think immigrants can find a balance then between assimilating the new culture and preserving their old?*

AC: I think food is very important to culture. The French place a big emphasis on food, and so do the Italians and the Chinese. I think it is very important that people keep their diet. They must eat at least one of their own meals a day. That's what I was brought up with. We had Chinese food every single night. My mother learned to cook it, and we had it every night. Even though we had chicken salad sandwiches to take to school at lunch, and chocolate cake when we came home from school, at night we always had Chinese food with a bowl of rice. Food is a very important way to keep in touch with the old country.

MG: *Do you think our Canadian ideal of a multicultural society is likely to work?*

AC: Oh, I think multiculturalism can work providing people understand that this is still Canada and it's founded on two founding nations - English and French - and it has an English common law system and a constitution that's based on the Magna Carta in Britain. If you understand that and don't think of it as a small, walled village somewhere in which you did what you wished, then it's fine. But I mean, you've got only yourself to blame if you behave like that, in an unacceptable manner. Mentally, you're never going to be happy. After all, there are things that are very valuable about this country. The reason why all those people from Hong Kong want to come here with all their money, for instance, is that this is a stable country. Why is it a stable country? Precisely because of all of these values that have been created over two hundred years here. People have contributed to that and to the political system and to everything, and if new immigrants don't take part in that they're making a big mistake.

▼▼▼▼▼▼▼▼▼

# *B*lack Like Me

■

F  I  L     F  R  A  S  E  R

*W*hen I was a careful boy growing up in Montreal, Canada was a country in which blacks like me developed an instinct about where we were welcome. Unlike the U.S., where racism was direct, Canada was, in its unsung way, more subtle. Here "discriminating" restaurants gave off a palpable hostility that seeped into your system as you sat at table, ignored. No one asked you to leave or told you to stay out, you were just not served. Across the border you could still see "No niggers" billboards, hand-lettered, which struck with a force that a new generation cannot understand.

We Frasers were in some ways more vulnerable since we didn't run with the pack - the pack being the black community centred on St. Antoine Street, not far from Windsor station where most heads of households worked as "red-caps" and conductors. My father, a student at McGill when he came to Canada in the 1920s, decided we should live away from what a later generation would describe as a ghetto. We went down to St. Antoine Street for haircuts and for semiannual visits to hear Reverend Este preach at the Negro church. But we lived in St. Leonard

■ ■ ■ ■ ■ ■ ■ ■ ■ ■ ■ ■ ■ ■ ■ ■ ■ ■ ■ ■ ■

Fil Fraser was born and raised in Montreal's east end. His reporting career has landed him jobs at radio stations across Canada. He now works for ACCESS, Alberta's educational television network.

de Port Maurice, a farming community abutting refinery row on the island's east end. The St. Antoine Street kids knew their turf and stuck to it. We experimented, and in the process developed sharp and useful reflexes.

The Montreal of my growing up was just as harsh on its majority culture, Francophones. English-speaking westenders, who saw no virtue in bilingualism, called them Frenchmen, usually with an alliterative expletive, or pea-soupers, or pepsis, the latter term making no sense to me, since I liked Pepsi too. The French kids also developed a sense about where they were welcome - west of the Ontario streetcar line, behind Morgan's department store, was territory to be careful in.

Those of us who belonged to minorities, visible or otherwise, knew what we were up against, put our heads down, and did the best we could. A boy in my class at Montreal High told me he couldn't get into McGill's medical school, even with first-class marks, because the quota for Jewish students that year had been filled. Amazingly (why would anyone want to go where he wasn't wanted?), there was a waiting list for Jews. Today, I hear, the man is a prominent politician, not a doctor.

In the early years of World War II, when I was not quite a teenager, marauding bands of English-Canadian soldiers roamed east-end Montreal, looking for Frenchies to beat up. That was after Mackenzie King capitulated and it was no longer "Not necessarily conscription, but conscription if necessary," and Mayor Camillien Houde was interned for heaping profanity on the idea of French Canadians' fighting the English war. Every so often an English-Canadian soldier was caught off base by a French gang. That was bad. But no one had it worse than the handful of French Canadians who had enlisted voluntarily.

Later, when the war was over and Montreal became "the Paris of North America," many of the displaced persons, "D.P.s" who had come to reinvent their lives, were doing well with new, anglicized names. But Eartha Kitt, the toast of Paris and New York, couldn't get into the Ritz. And the Caughnawaga Indians, rich in their ancient traditions, were just another local tourist attraction.

There were variations on the theme as you crossed the country. We had heard, without great surprise, about the internment of Japanese

Canadians in the west. After all, we had Germans locked up along with Camillien Houde. Every now and then some of the scandal sheets would flash headlines about the Ku Klux Klan somewhere out near Moose Jaw going after Catholics, and the better-informed French Canadians, almost always Catholic, knew about Ontario's Orangemen. Ukrainians were *out* in Edmonton, Germans were *out* in Winnipeg. Across the country who was out varied from place to place. Who was *in* never changed. To be of British descent was to have access to the corridors of power and prestige. Everybody else tried to join in. We all sang "God Save the King" and saluted the Union Jack.

Canada was a "white man's country" - as Mackenzie King put it in 1908, when he was deputy minister of labour. The phrase became the title of a book by Ted Ferguson. "That Canada should remain a white man's country," Ferguson quotes the future prime minister as saying, "is . . . not only desirable for economic and social reasons but highly necessary on political and national grounds." That meant a white, Anglo-Saxon, Protestant, man's country. It never occurred to us, then, what that meant to women. Our immigration policy, pragmatic since "les filles du roi," was to bring in Chinese to do the dirty work of building the railroad, and central and eastern Europeans with their sheepskins to fill up the Prairies and create business for the railroad. The policy did not include giving the immigrants any real piece of the Canadian action.

And yet, astonishingly, Canada today is unique in the world, embracing and encouraging more diversity than any other country. We are officially, and by degrees viscerally, a multicultural country. The British are a minority, and beginning to act like it. Multiculturalism is enshrined in the Canadian Charter of Rights and Freedoms, is reflected in our institutions, and is seeping, far more rapidly than we realize, into our collective psyche. Canada has become a country that says its citizens are equal, regardless of race, or religion, or origin, or age, or physical or mental status, or sex. The courts back up that idea, it seems, almost weekly.

How did this happen? I don't remember any politician running a campaign on the virtues of multiculturalism - at least not until the very recent past. No government has been elected on the promise of settling the debt with the natives, or making the country safe for boat people. And yet the mould is made, and set. No politician, no government, can now dismantle the charter, the institutions, the labour agreements, the judicial precedents that make us the only truly open, multicultural country in the world.

I suppose I'm as typically Canadian as anyone. I was born in Montreal. My father came from Trinidad, a scholarship student who chose not to go back to help his country; my mother was born on a Canadian ship, inbound from Barbados, about to dock in Montreal. That puts me in roughly the same situation as a third of Canadians, belonging to neither of the so-called founding peoples.

I think the ferment began as we entered the 1960s. Diefenbaker was in Ottawa, having been given considerable assistance by a waning but still potent Maurice Duplessis. Jean Lesage, following hard on Duplessis' heels with the same objectives but a different style, set the Quiet Revolution in motion, with spectacular success. No one now disputes whether Francophones can claim to be *maîtres chez nous.* Tommy Douglas was in Regina running the first socialist government in North America.

For reasons that had nothing to do with politics, I moved from Montreal to Regina in 1958. The next year a local firm, Queen City Real Estate, refused to rent an apartment to me. Not many years earlier, in Montreal, I would have shrugged, told myself that my reflexes were getting rusty, and moved on to the next listing. But there was something different now about the Canadian atmosphere, and about me. I found out quickly and easily from an embarrassed clerk that Queen City had a "whites only" rental policy. My reaction was interesting - not anger, or fear, or shame. Rather it was a welcome opportunity to right a wrong, summed up simply as "You can't do that in this country." Any more. Saskatchewan had passed a bill of rights, and "The Queen vs. Queen City Real Estate" was the first case of discrimination tried under the legislation. The attorney general insisted that the crown, not the complainant, lay the charge; and with little fanfare, Queen City was found guilty and fined. It offered me an apartment, which I declined.

I met John Diefenbaker in the early 1960s, mainstreeting in Prince Albert. How easily politicians moved about in those days! Dief, full of righteous vitality, was out for a walk down a road that was really called Main Street, shaking hands and talking to the people with no entourage and no bodyguards. When he shook my hand I felt genuine warmth, which I returned. As a reporter, I had covered the 1958 election for radio station CFCF in Montreal with appropriate cynicism, nearly getting punched by George Hees when I asked him about the Diefenbaker-Duplessis axis which delivered the Tory landslide in Quebec.

But I felt that Diefenbaker's 1960 Canadian Bill of Rights had been a mile-stone for Canada. It redeemed him in my mind for the alliance with Duplessis, who these days is being given a revised place in history as a defender of Quebec autonomy. But in my time in Montreal he was known, among other things, as the author of the Padlock Law, used as a legal bludgeon against Jehovah's Witnesses in Quebec under the guise of fighting communism.

I had argued in favour of the Bill of Rights, with all its limitations. It was not entrenched in the constitution and it applied only to federal law. It could be dismissed, as it was by J.D. Morton in *Saturday Night* in September, 1960, as "a lawyer's tool." I remember well the arguments that the bill would limit rather than enlarge human rights already, opponents said, effectively guaranteed under British common law. The bill would open loopholes, it was full of escape clauses. It could even be superseded by the War Measures Act. And so on. With the passage of the bill, Canadians, for the first time, could not be discriminated against on the basis of race, colour, or creed. The bill moved individual rights out of British common law and into hard legislation.

The Royal Commission on Bilingualism and Biculturalism came officially face to face, for the first time in our history, with the fact that there was an important minority in Canada of neither British nor French descent. In the commission's report the term "multiculturalism" first assumed the status of hard currency. The other day I came across a brochure I had saved announcing a conference on multiculturalism for Canada in August, 1970, at the University of Alberta. The conference was opened by Senator Paul Yuzyk, and I, wearing as one of my hats the programme directorship of Canada's first educational television station, got a half-hour to talk about multiculturalism in broadcasting. The back of the programme listed the sixteen recommendations in book four of the B & B Commission, "The Cultural Contribution of the Other Ethnic Groups."

Jean Lesage's clarion call to an awakening French Canada did much more than give Francophones a new sense of themselves. It stirred the aspirations of minorities in other provinces. If Francophones in Quebec could get out from under the British hegemony, what about Ukrainians in Alberta, Italians in Toronto, Chinese in Vancouver, and Indians everywhere?

And there were the thousands who, when they encountered discrimination, began slowly to realize, as I did, that "You can't do that in this country, any more" - and found the laws backed them up. Many who had come in waves of postwar immigration - from Hungary and Czechoslovakia and Poland, from Bangladesh and Uganda, from the United States during the Vietnam war, from the East and West Indies, and later from southeast Asia - didn't come here to be second-class citizens or part of a melting pot. They came to what they perceived as a compassionate country. Few other nations had opened their doors as Canada did. And the remnant of racism and discrimination they found, now with no legal, institutional, or moral base, was ripe for attack.

In many parts of Canada the attack is now in full flood. But even though the outcome of the war seems inevitable, no one should believe that all the battles have been won. While those of us who have been here for a generation or more usually find a comfortable niche, it's still tough to be a new immigrant in Canada. And while there are some who see a future in which we double our present population with new immigration, there are also those who continue to fight the rearguard action. For all the usual reasons: they'll take our jobs - they won't adapt to our system - they'll only bring another country's problems to our shores - they'll spoil our way of life.

In a series of articles under the heading "A Minority Report," the *Toronto Star* illustrated "the Metro mosaic." More than 100 minority groups, who make up a majority of the population, still face prejudice, hidden and unhidden. Some kids today, as I did in the 1930s and

1940s, have to fight their way home from school. Still, we've come a long way from the days when immigrants were greeted with signs that proclaimed "no dogs or Jews allowed."

In 1986 the minister of justice, John Crosbie, told the House of Commons that the government was committed to ending discrimination that keeps individuals in Canada from fully realizing their potential, and embraced its duty to take the lead in making sure that federal laws and policies met the high standards of the charter and that individuals were not forced unnecessarily into court.

In a speech last April in Toronto, the then minister of state for multiculturalism, Otto Jelinek, was able to say, "Our society has become *irreversibly* multicultural and multiracial," even though he had still not resolved the question of an apology and honourable compensation for the wartime insult to Japanese Canadians. And the prime minister, speaking to the same gathering, issued what might well have been the slogan for multiculturalism in the 1980s. "Tokenism is over," he said. "Fairness is in."

Our record, in the years after World War II, stands in stark contrast to a long and shameful series of events culminating with the internment of Japanese and German Canadians in the 1940s. In 1903 the government of Canada raised the head tax on Chinese immigrants, originally established at $50 in 1885, to $500. In 1914, a boatload of 376 Indian refugees was refused permission to land in Vancouver, and suffered incredible privation because we were stingy, to put it kindly, about giving them food and water. In 1939, 907 Jews escaping Nazi Germany aboard the *St. Louis* were refused entry to Canada. At the time, Hitler's attempted genocide was in full flood.

Canada's postwar immigrants landed with a painful awareness of war and racism. After they found their feet in this new land, they weren't about to put up with more. There was little to be done about private prejudice but, as the law developed, in provincial and federal jurisdictions, it said that public services were equally available to all.

It was, ironically, Pierre Trudeau who finished the legal transformation that John Diefenbaker, for whom he had only disdain, had started. The full-bodied reverberations from the act of patriation and the enshrinement of the charter in the Canadian constitution will be felt beyond the next generation. Canada's first ombudsman, George McClelland, a former commissioner of the RCMP, was appointed by the government of Alberta in 1967. By 1986 all provinces except Prince Edward Island had established such an office. Now, not only did human-rights legislation have teeth, but a publicly funded defender. Individual rights in Canada no longer depend upon some vaguely defined and unevenly interpreted "common law." Our most "uncommon" laws (if you look around the world) are meeting the tests of the courts, as precedent upon precedent builds a legal and moral base.

It's somehow typical that we Canadians have difficulty recognizing our uniqueness. We see ourselves as a not very powerful, not very innovative, not very exciting land that is nevertheless safe. We look to other countries with envy, wishing we had their strength, their depth of culture and character, their creativity.

But look more closely. Our first motherland, France, is culturally stagnant, lurching from political to economic to social crisis. Britain, once the home of empire, is in danger of losing its role as leader of the Commonwealth. Its immigration policy is a shambles; its class society still flourishes; its problems with Ireland defy solution. And when we look, nervously, at our continental neighbour, our desire to buy into the American dream becomes highly selective. The melting pot never really worked - yet in the United States multiculturalism is a very recent notion. Everyone - the Puerto Ricans, the Indians, the Mexicans, the various other Latinos - is "American", whether they like it or not.

In the Middle East, the cradle of civilization, even brothers can't get along. Beirut, once one of the world's most sophisticated cities, is a war zone. In Israel, Jews attack Jews, desecrating synagogues. India is still trying to grapple with racial and religious strife, even though untouchability is officially dead. China is working at being homogeneous. In the Soviet Union some are more equal than others. The Swiss are multicultural, but only for the four official groups. Most of the world's countries are either unicultural, uniracial, and religiously homogeneous, or else caught up in internal strife.

It's not hard to understand why the notion of multiculturalism is so difficult, and why so few countries have contemplated adopting the ideal as policy. It is, first of all, risky. When you allow people to emigrate from other countries and keep their cultures, their ties to former countries, you invite ancient rivalries and hatreds to settle into the land. The hope is that old hurts and fears will mellow as those people find a measure of security in a benign environment - and the Canadian experience has, by and large, borne this out.

But multiculturalism, with its implicit ties to other cultures, also obviates narrow nationalism. In a way, you ride the fine line between being an open, free, and tolerant society, and not really being a country at all, at least in the "My country right or wrong" sense. The gamble is that in the end there is pride in tolerance; that a new kind of nationhood, safer in a tinderbox world, can be built on the open international communication that comes with multiculturalism. As Eric Hoffer noted of the "true believer," those who most loudly protest, defend, and propagate the faith are those who are the least secure in it. Nations that feel threatened, uncertain of their morality, become aggressive and dangerous.

How then to explain Canada's behaviour? Does the moral authority flowing from our compassionate immigration policy, from our record in foreign aid, from Pearson's Nobel Peace Prize or Trudeau's international stardom, give a kind of courage? Is there some special serenity, some security that stems from knowing that multiculturalism, while not easy, works? Not only are we comfortable with the extraordinary diversity of our peoples, we plan expansion on the same basis. Major political parties are now arguing not about where new immigrants will come from, or what their colour or creed will be, but about how many we can absorb, and how soon.

Canadians have yet to discover the creativity of their social order. If we can solve the problems of making it possible for people of every kind to live together in reasonable harmony, we have a message for the world. The problems of this shrinking planet are problems we're solving in Canada.

When I was invited to a mainstream event in the 1950s it was because I was exotic. In the sixties and seventies I was often the token black. But in the eighties when they call, I know it's really me they want. Not bad for a kid who grew up in east-end Montreal thinking someone had put him on the wrong planet.

▼▼▼▼▼▼▼▼▼▼

# *R*ebirth

■

P A B L O     U R B A N Y I

Ottawa, 27 August 198...

ear Alberto,

I really must apologize for not replying at once to that letter you sent me more than two years ago. There are many, though not countless, reasons for the delay. On the one hand, living in this wonderful world of global communications, I often found myself saying: "Hell, why bother to write? When you've got something to say, you just hop on a plane and fly down there and tell him all about it over a cup of coffee." I realize now that you can say that to yourself for two or three years, maybe even a lifetime, while you sit and wait for the money for the ticket. On the other hand, with all due respect, you must admit that your letter is full of dumb questions about the food, the customs, the clothing and the climate - the kind of things you can find out about in any good tourist guidebook in greater detail than I could ever provide. Then you ask me about the people, and right at the end

■ ■ ■ ■ ■ ■ ■ ■ ■ ■ ■ ■ ■ ■ ■ ■ ■ ■ ■ ■

Although Pablo Urbanyi was born in Hungary, he grew up in Argentina. He worked as a journalist and a cultural commentator before coming to Canada in 1977. He has written two novels, *Un revolver para Mack* and *The Nowhere Idea*, as well as a collection of short stories titled *Noche de Revolucionaires*. Urbanyi now lives in Ottawa.

you ask after me, how I am and how I'm getting on in Canada.

What can I tell you about the people? Society here is organized in such a way that from the time you're born you can fend for yourself. People practically don't matter. But since you ask I could describe the people (today's people, "post-modern people" they should be termed since here what's modern is passé: everything is "post-") by quoting a local poet who knows more about these things than I do. In a long poem depicting a remote past in which man, happily and without prejudice, ate raw meat and never had any cavities, this writer defines his contemporaries in a parody of Kipling's poem "If": "If you get up early in the morning and return home in the evening to get drunk . . . If you watch T.V. for three hours while you get drunk . . . If you have doubts and seek information on the latest sexual techniques, on today's God, on microwave cooking . . . If you pay your bills regularly . . . If you are taken in by special offers and dutifully buy everything they tell you to . . . If you use bathroom tissue correctly . . . If you don't know where you came from or who you are or where you're going . . . You will be a post-modern man, faceless in the crowd."

The final vision of the poem is truly apocalyptic: all humanity plunges into the abyss, each man carrying the brand of the beast on his forehead (which in this case does not symbolize Rome but the United States).

I look at it in the same way that you probably do. What the poet thinks is only one opinion among many. Man today doesn't need lofty truths but rather immediate answers to his daily problems, categoric replies and drastic solutions to the life he drags along the ground behind him. It would never occur to post-modern man to hold a skull in his hand and pose an unanswerable question. He would rather brandish a toilet roll with pride and exclaim: "Eureka! I've found it!" And stuffing it under his arm or dumping it into his supermarket cart, he would continue on his way, brimming with confidence, common sense, positive thinking, optimism, every inch a man of action, repeating at every step "Everything's fine".

From what I've said so far, you should be getting the picture. Speaking about myself and about how I'm getting on, you shouldn't still think in terms of the person I used to be. You've got to think of me as someone who adapted and was born again. So in this letter I'm going to outline briefly the metamorphosis I underwent, and I'll leave for another day the description of the effects of that change on my daily life. I can tell you already, though, that my next letter will be entitled "One Day in the Life of Pavlov Urbanovitch in the Ottawa Gulag". Ottawa is the city I live in at the moment.

When I arrived here I naively thought that having been a Hungarian immigrant in Argentina at the age of eight and having grown up in Buenos Aires, I was an old hand at the game and had seen it all, so that managing a second bout of immigration would be a piece of cake. I thought I would take the world by storm. How wrong can you be! There's been a good deal of progress in the meantime. Just think: the Americans have put a man on the moon.

I was unable to get very far with my great powers of deductive reasoning and theoretical speculation or with my desire to fashion in the air a better, more harmonious, efficient, organized world, with every little thing in its rightful place. It was there in front of me, but I couldn't see it. I had to shelve my elaborate theories worked out in cafés and humbly accept what was there. In other words. I had to experience, to soak up experience. There's a good deal of sense in the Latin saying "*Experientia docet stultus*" (Experience is the teacher of idiots).

There are a lot of things I could tell you - about the doors here and the trouble I had getting them open; or the taps they have, in so many different shapes and sizes, and the times I soaked myself before I figured out how to use them properly; or how, like a fool, I used to say hello to women in the street I'd never met before because they all looked alike to me, with the same hairstyle and make-up, all dolled up in the latest fashions which make them look extremely attractive and totally unique - a far cry from the grey uniformity you see in underdeveloped or communist countries. Yes, my friend, everything is bright and cheerful here. But let me give you a concrete example instead of rambling on like this.

Let's begin with man, man going about his daily business with a roll of toilet tissue in his hand and a question in his mind: "Is it or isn't it?"

This was the situation I found myself in for the first time one day, propping up my cart in the Supermarket, the Cathedral of Consumerism, opposite the High Altar of Bathroom Tissue, attempting, without experience or knowledge, to perform the daily rite: shopping.

Oh ignorance! Life in this world is a good deal richer and more varied than some simple-minded architects of utopias would have us believe. People actually live in Utopia here. I was struck dumb as I surveyed with awe the rolls of bathroom tissue that rose upwards like organ pipes toward heaven. How can I explain it to you or describe the scene? Words fail me. But I know I'm no poet, so I won't try to wax too lyrical. I'll just paint the basic picture, starting with the colours: daffodil yellow, flesh pink and sky blue, from the lightest to the darkest hue of cream, any colour to match your bathroom décor (I only found out about this later), and classical white like the purest driven snow. There were specialized tissues too - tissues for dogs, tissues for cats, tissues for your most intimate needs. Then there were the printed tissues - with pictures of Bambi and the whole Disney menagerie for children; pictures of Hollywood stars ( I can't remember if Ronald Reagan was among them) and scenes from recent films for adolescents; pictures of Japanese (or maybe Chinese) rural scenes and reproductions of Renaissance paintings for people with artistic sensibility; pictures of vintage cars for the casualties of fashion overcome with nostalgia. And all these came in a variety of different qualities: tough or extra-tough, soft or extra-soft (for people with hemorrhoids); one-ply, two-ply, three-ply; smooth or pleated . . . . I won't go on because you'll think I'm making it up.

I felt like Dante in the Black Forest searching for his Virgil. The shock was so great on this first encounter that I ended up buying nothing. And that was as much a crime against society as it was against my family sitting at home waiting for me.

But God came to my rescue, and I found some other Argentinian emigrés who acted as my Virgil and pointed me in the right direction. There was a psychoanalyst, a doctor and three university professors, one of literature, one of economics, and the other of philosophy. They all agreed that "Hey, in Argentina there isn't any bathroom tissue at all," and that this was a good reason for continuing to live in this part of the world. They understood my problem perfectly since they'd had it at one time themselves, and generously got together one evening to help me solve it. The psychoanalyst, who's as fat as a barrel and sat there the whole time with a bag of candy in his hand, avoided any uncouth interpretations and was encouraging: "Don't forget that you came here to indulge in certain luxuries and pleasures. Buy whichever one you like best and gives you the greatest satisfaction. Personally, I always buy the cheapest make, except when I get constipated and tied up in a vicious circle full of anxiety. I speak from experience." And with that, he popped a candy into his mouth. I asked the doctor about the different colours and the problem of hygiene and he explained: "Listen, as soon as you step foot in North America you've got to stop thinking like that and start generalizing. It's true that I have come across the odd case of a nasty allergic reaction, but they've been very infrequent and exceptional. Generally speaking, the colours tend not to run and you should have faith in American technology. My advice to you is to test carefully, little by little, and if you notice the slightest reaction, change colour." The economics professor took a different line: "Look, it'll be worth your while. Sit down with your family and work out how much you use per day, per week, per month and per year. That way you'll have a clear idea of your overall budget. Oh yes, and to make allowances for diarrhea, you just apply the theory of possibilities." The professor of philosophy, as bald as Socrates, sighed: "What can I say? In my opinion, the ideal bathroom tissue hasn't been made yet. Perhaps in another world, in a different social system . . . ." "And what kind of tissue would that be?" I asked. "Well, em, er, the recyclable kind, well . . . of course . . . ."

Before I go on and in order not to hurt your patriotic feelings by getting into pointless arguments about whether or not there is bathroom tissue down there and if it's available on the black market like the dollar, I should point out that I only take the opinion as a spontaneous exclamation brought about by the biased division established by developed countries when they communicate with the underdeveloped ones. This division could be rendered into everyday language by "Countries with clean backsides and countries with dirty backsides". So much so that many North American diplomats (who, since they have no bidet in their own homes, cannot conceive that there could be one in someone else's in another part of the world and so find the tissue problem truly alarming; I do too) cram their suitcases with as many rolls as they think they'll need when they visit a third-world country. Now I can go on.

Do you think I was any the happier having received these initial clarifications? Not on your life. I was still overwhelmed with doubts and uncertainties. My hand still trembled when I reached out to tear off a sheet of paper and I couldn't avoid accidents. My helpers - unwittingly, of course - in their eagerness to demonstrate their individuality, their ability to fend for themselves and to affirm their personalities, forgot to advise me on the scientific aspects of the problem. They overlooked the need to establish the kind of solid intellectual foundation and impeccable background, based on research, that would enable a person to make his way through that jungle on the right path. There's no religion on earth that has life *that* carefully worked out and lacks its mindless mysteries!

And as happens with all great discoveries that alter one's destiny, I also discovered, by accident or by chance, the solution to the problem. One day I was passing a newspaper stand and noticed a magazine called *Perfect Consumer.* It was a non-profit publication, pure and uncontaminated (a true rarity in this world), and contained a section entitled "The latest tests on bathroom tissues currently available". Full of expectation, I bought a copy.

I would only bore you if I gave you the names of all the toilet tissues and listed all the data given on the subject. I reckon you would need a lifetime or a course or to have been born here in order to understand it all. So I'll just go straight to the conclusions presented in the main article. These were written in a straightforward intelligible style (you can't complain here because they always take your mental capacity into account so as to guarantee effective communication) and read as follows: "Headed by the world renowned eminent scientist John Haighsmith, 46 and father of three, a team of experts from the prestigious University of Toronto undertook three months of intensive research financed by this magazine (at a total cost of $38,000.00) using a series of specially designed tests (there's no description of the tests or of the methodology used) and came to an indisputable conclusion concerning bathroom tissues currently available on the market: in comparison with Kitten X2-X2, Tiger XX-X1, Romance XX-X2, Intimacy

XX-X3, and Passion ZZ-Z1, Swan XZ-Z1, being two-ply and manufactured with original, non-recycled cellulose, is the safest and most reliable tissue available. Despite the high price of Swan XZ-Z1, over an average period of ten years the consumer stands to make the most substantial savings by virtue of the lower rate of tears and related mishaps. It should also be borne in mind that, according to the reports generously submitted by the Ontario Medical Association, the white variety of Swan is the most sterile and hygienic, accounting for the lowest number of recorded cases of allergic reaction. (Unfortunately, the consumer will have to forego pleasure of matching his interior design or of putting that finishing touch to his bathroom décor or whatever other fantasies he might have). Consequently, this is the only bathroom tissue recommended by the O.M.A., not to invalidate the money-back guarantee, readers are advised to study the instructions concerning the correct use of Swan tissue in the box on the preceding page."

I reckon that with this example (that could be applied to any other of a thousand products, from toothpaste to condoms) I've put you in the picture. I can assure you that at last I have found true happiness, I feel that my inner self has been strengthened, my individuality has blossomed and my entire personality moves with greater conviction along the path I'm following.

I know more about the subject than anybody now and can speak about it with confidence. My hand no longer trembles as it reaches out to tear off a sheet. My fears have vanished. And if I sometimes think that there's a little swan swimming down there ready to peck me, or a kitten ready to sink its claws into me, I can't blame society or the commercials on T.V. that use these animals. The problem is in my mind where I tend to make these free associations rather too easily.

At any rate, experience has confirmed the findings of experts, and I can now be proud of fending for myself.

Best wishes
Pablo

P.S. I almost forgot. Are you still thinking about emigrating over here? It's true, as you say, that things are easier to buy here. While you're making up your mind and to make it a bit easier for you, I can send you a pack of Swan with eight rolls in it, which is the most economical way of buying it. The best way of sending it, I think, is by diplomatic bag if I can get hold of an Argentinian diplomat going home or a Canadian who's being posted there. Let me know what you think.

▼▼▼▼▼▼▼▼▼

# *A Boat Girl Grows Up*

■

B   A   R   R   Y       C   A   M   E

*E*ven after 10 years, there are memories that make Hang Truong wince. Among them is the recollection of one of the first mornings in her new home in Coldwater, an Ontario town of 1,000 on the banks of a river of the same name, not far from Orillia. The townspeople, in a gesture of welcome, had donated a bicycle. So Hang did what she would have done in her native Saigon. The result was not what she expected. "I think they were a little scandalized," she recalled with a shy smile. "I guess we were," agreed Jane Walker, a lifelong resident of Coldwater. "We just weren't accustomed to seeing a 20-year-old girl riding around on a bicycle in her pyjamas." The young woman was part of the wave of Southeast Asian Boat People who found haven in Canada.

Hang is now a mother and a budding entrepreneur. And the town that opened its arms to her is no longer quite so surprised by peculiar foreign habits and customs. As Walker, one of a group of four

Barry Came was born in London, England in 1943. He came to Canada in 1948, and grew up in Toronto. He travelled extensively for a number of years as foreign correspondent for *Newsweek* magazine. Came now lives in Toronto, and works as a writer for *Maclean's*. He has written two novels, *Rice Wine* and *Pirate Coast*, and is working on a third.

▼▼▼▼▼▼▼▼▼

Coldwater families who sponsored Hang and two of her young cousins, remarked: "It was very good for our little community here. It really broadened our horizons. In a place like this, you know, contact with people of other races is not something that happens every day."

For Hang, it was a contact that might never have occurred if Prime Minister Joe Clark's newly elected Conservative government had not committed itself to help the Boat People in 1979. Most of them, like Hang, were ethnic Chinese who had fled from Vietnam after the fall of Saigon in 1975. Clark's administration encouraged private-sector volunteerism, with the government at first matching each refugee that individuals and church groups agreed to support, up to a total of 50,000 - in the end, 60,049 Boat People landed in Canada by the end of 1980. The program led four Coldwater families, with the aid of United Church minister Rev. John Allsop, to form a sponsoring group. They notified Ottawa that they were prepared to sponsor a Vietnamese family, specifying that they would take individuals with a low priority who might not otherwise have a chance of admission to Canada.

Hang was in that category. She was 20, unmarried, with no relatives in Canada, no knowledge of English or French and not particularly well educated. In Vietnam, she had helped her foster mother run a food stall in the market at Cholon, the teeming Chinese ghetto in the heart of Saigon. What is more, she had in her care her two young cousins - Ong Vi Truong, 8, and his brother Ming, 15. All three had spent more than a year in a Malaysian refugee camp on Pulau Bidong, a tiny island in the Gulf of Thailand, with 56,000 other refugees.

They had reached the camp after spending six days at sea on a 23-foot wooden boat crammed with 508 Vietnamese fleeing from their homeland. The trip, like that experienced by most of the Boat People, had been dangerous. Thai pirates attacked the boat on five separate occasions. Although Hang was not physically abused by the attackers, they robbed her of all the valuables she had been carrying - including jewelry and $2,000 in U.S. currency that she had sewn into the seam of her brassiere. Said Hang: "I was destitute. I didn't know what I was going to do or where I was going to go, and on top of everything else, I had the two boys to look after."

It was while the small family languished in Malaysia that fate, in the form of the Coldwater sponsors, intervened. The four principal families involved, besides undertaking to care for Hang and the boys for a year, had also pooled their resources to make a down payment on an $18,000 bungalow. Others in the town gave money and worked on refurbishing the house. "It was a real community effort," said Harold Wood, one of the four main sponsors. Added Hang: "I had not even applied to go to Canada. I knew nothing about this country. I did not know the language. I did not know my sponsors. I did not know where I was going. I was very, very scared." Said Wood, who met Hang and the two boys when they arrived at Toronto airport: "I think she was terrified."

The fear passed, however, and it was replaced by a quality that some Coldwater residents found almost as unsettling. "She worked awfully hard," said Wood's wife, Inga, herself a wartime refugee from Yugoslavia. "There were moments when I was worried that she might be trying to do too much." Hang was soon holding down two jobs, working 10 hours a day at a Coldwater florist and at a local nursing home. At the same time, she was looking after the two boys, who were enrolled in Coldwater schools, as well as finding the time to attend her own English-language courses in Orillia, 20 km away. In her class, she met Du Truong, another Vietnamese refugee who had arrived in Canada a week after she had. Two years later, they were married.

The wedding was a social event in Coldwater, providing both an illustration of how completely the local people had accepted Hang and how acclimatized she had become to her new home. She was married at the United Church. For the ceremony she wore a traditional Western white gown. After the ceremony, she changed into a traditional Chinese red silk dress. As Walker remarked, "It was marvellous, a combination of everything good about Canada and China."

Eventually, the couple achieved modest prosperity. Hang continued to work, and her husband found a job at a Coldwater plant manufacturing plastic garbage bags. They soon took over the mortgage payments for the bungalow that their sponsors had bought, eventually purchasing the house. They also had three children. Said Hang: "I got married, and every year after that I produced a baby."

The children did not slow her pace. Five years after arriving in

Canada, Hang and her family sold the Coldwater house and moved to Orillia. "I hated to leave," she said, "but Du got a job as a grinder in an automobile parts plant and, anyway, we're not that far away." The couple now owns a modest but handsome $55,000 home in Orillia. They are partners with Du's brother in owning a small block of furnished apartments. And later this month, Hang and a Chinese girlfriend, an immigrant from Hong Kong, will open a snack bar in Orillia. Said Hang: "We're calling it 'Genie'. It's magic, like the magic that brought me here."

Canada has also been kind to the two young boys who accompanied Hang. Ming, the eldest, is now married and living in Toronto. Ong has remained with Hang, where his hockey, baseball and badminton trophies decorate the living room in the family's home. He is scheduled to graduate from the Orillia District Collegiate and Vocational Institute next year, after which he hopes to study fashion design at Ryerson Polytechnic Institute in Toronto. He has no regrets about the move to this country, even though he does not recall much about the trials he underwent to arrive here. "All I can remember is that I was scared, all of the time," he said.

Hang's original sponsors are clearly delighted with her success. Said Walker: "We certainly got a wonderful family, and they have done wonderfully well." At the same time, however, even those who were directly involved in getting Hang to Canada say that they are not sure if the process could ever be repeated. Added Wood: "I doubt whether it would be as easy now. The whole climate here has changed." Said his wife, Inga: "I don't think Canadians are any less generous than they used to be. But they are certainly much more ambivalent now about the whole issue of immigration."

▼▼▼▼▼▼▼▼▼

# The Management of Grief

■

## BHARATI MUKHERJEE

A woman I don't know is boiling tea the Indian way in my kitchen. There are a lot of women I don't know in my kitchen, whispering, and moving tactfully. They open doors, rummage through the pantry, and try not to ask me where things are kept. They remind me of when my sons were small, on Mother's Day or when Vikram and I were tired, and they would make big, sloppy omelets. I would lie in bed pretending I didn't hear them.

Dr. Sharma, the treasurer of the Indo-Canada Society, pulls me into the hallway. He wants to know if I am worried about money. His wife, who has just come up from the basement with a tray of empty cups and glasses, scolds him. "Don't bother Mrs. Bhave with mundane details." She looks so monstrously pregnant her baby must be days overdue. I tell her she shouldn't be carrying heavy things. "Shaila," she says, smiling, "this is the fifth." Then she grabs a teenager by his shirttails. He slips his Walkman off his head. He has to be one of her four children,

■ ■ ■ ■ ■ ■ ■ ■ ■ ■ ■ ■ ■ ■ ■ ■ ■ ■ ■ ■ ■

Bharati Mukherjee was born in Calcutta, India. She has written two novels, a travel memoir, and two collections of short stories, most recently, *The Middleman And Other Stories*. Associating Canada with painful memories of expatriation, she now lives with her husband, writer Clark Blaise, in Iowa City, Iowa (U.S.A).

they have the same domed and dented foreheads. "What's the official word now?" she demands. The boy slips the headphones back on. "They're acting evasive, Ma. They're saying it could be an accident or a terrorist bomb."

All morning, the boys have been muttering, Sikh Bomb, Sikh Bomb. The men, not using the word, bow their heads in agreement. Mrs. Sharma touches her forehead at such a word. At least they've stopped talking about space debris and Russian lasers.

Two radios are going in the dining room. They are tuned to different stations. Someone must have brought the radios down from my boys' bedrooms. I haven't gone into their rooms since Kusum came running across the front lawn in her bathrobe. She looked so funny, I was laughing when I opened the door.

The big TV in the den is being whizzed through American networks and cable channels.

"Damn!" some man swears bitterly. "How can these preachers carry on like nothing's happened?" I want to tell him we're not that important. You look at the audience, and at the preacher in his blue robe with his beautiful white hair, the potted palm trees under a blue sky, and you know they care about nothing.

The phone rings and rings. Dr. Sharma's taken charge. "We're with her," he keeps saying. "Yes, yes, the doctor has given calming pills. Yes, yes, pills are having necessary effect." I wonder if pills alone explain this calm. Not peace, just a deadening quiet. I was always controlled, but never repressed. Sound can reach me, but my body is tensed, ready to scream. I hear their voices all around me. I hear my boys and Vikram cry, "Mommy, Shaila!" and their screams insulate me, like headphones.

The woman boiling water tells her story again and again. "I got the news first. My cousin called from Halifax before six A.M., can you imagine? He'd gotten up for prayers and his son was studying for medical exams and he heard on a rock channel that something had happened to a plane. They said first it had disappeared from the radar, like a giant eraser just reached out. His father called me, so I said to him, what do you mean, 'something bad'? You mean a hijacking? And he said, *behn*, there is no confirmation of anything yet, but check with your neighbours because a lot of them must be on that plane. So I called poor

Kusum straightaway. I knew Kusum's husband and daughter were booked to go yesterday."

Kusum lives across the street from me. She and Satish had moved in less than a month ago. They said they needed a bigger place. All these people, the Sharmas and friends from the Indo-Canada Society had been there for the housewarming. Satish and Kusum made homemade tandoori on their big gas grill and even the white neighbours piled their plates high with that luridly red, charred, juicy chicken. Their younger daughter had danced, and even our boys had broken away from the Stanley Cup telecast to put in a reluctant appearance. Everyone took pictures for their albums and for the community newspapers - another of our families had made it big in Toronto - and now I wonder how many of those happy faces are gone. "Why does God give us so much if all along He intends to take it away?" Kusum asks me.

I nod. We sit on carpeted stairs, holding hands like children. "I never once told him that I loved him," I say. I was too much the well brought up woman. I was so well brought up I never felt comfortable calling my husband by his first name.

"It's all right," Kusum says. "He knew. My husband knew. They felt it. Modern young girls have to say it because what they feel is fake."

Kusum's daughter, Pam, runs in with an overnight case. Pam's in her McDonald's uniform. "Mummy! You have to get dressed!" Panic makes her cranky. "A reporter's on his way here."

"Why?"

"You want to talk to him in your bathrobe?" She starts to brush her mother's long hair. She's the daughter who's always in trouble. She dates Canadian boys and hangs out in the mall, shopping for tight sweaters. The younger one, the goody-goody one according to Pam, the one with a voice so sweet that when she sang *bhajans* for Ethiopian relief even a frugal man like my husband wrote out a hundred dollar check, *she* was on that plane. *She* was going to spend July and August with grandparents because Pam wouldn't go. Pam said she'd rather waitress at McDonald's. "If it's a choice between Bombay and Wonderland, I'm picking Wonderland," she'd said.

"Leave me alone," Kusum yells. "You know what I want to do? If I didn't have to look after you now, I'd hang myself."

Pam's young face goes blotchy with pain. "Thanks," she says, "don't let me stop you."

"Hush," pregnant Mrs. Sharma scolds Pam. "Leave your mother alone. Mr. Sharma will tackle the reporters and fill out the forms. He'll say what has to be said."

Pam stands her ground. "You think I don't know what Mummy's thinking? *Why her?* that's what. That's sick! Mummy wishes my little sister were alive and I were dead."

Kusum's hand in mine is trembly hot. We continue to sit on the stairs.

She calls before she arrives, wondering if there's anything I need. Her name is Judith Templeton and she's an appointee of the provincial government. "Multiculturalism?" I ask, and she says, "partially," but that her mandate is bigger. "I've been told you knew many of the people on the flight," she says. "Perhaps if you'd agree to help us reach the others . . . ?"

She gives me time at least to put on tea water and pick up the mess in the front room. I have a few *samosas* from Kusum's housewarming that I could fry up, but then I think, why prolong this visit?

Judith Templeton is much younger than she sounded. She wears a blue suit with a white blouse and a polka dot tie. Her blond hair is cut short, her only jewelry is pearl drop earrings. Her briefcase is new and expensive looking, a gleaming cordovan leather. She sits with it across her lap. When she looks out the front windows onto the street, her contact lenses seem to float in front of her light blue eyes.

"What sort of help do you want from me?" I ask. She has refused the tea, out of politeness, but I insist, along with some slightly stale biscuits.

"I have no experience," she admits. "That is, I have an MSW and I've worked in liaison with accident victims, but I mean I have no experience with a tragedy of this scale -"

"Who could?" I ask.

" - and with the complications of culture, language, and customs. Someone mentioned that Mrs. Bhave is a pillar - because you've taken it more calmly."

At this, perhaps, I frown, for she reaches forward, almost to take my hand. "I hope you understand my meaning, Mrs. Bhave. There are hundreds of people in Metro directly affected, like you, and some of them speak no English. There are some widows who've never handled money or gone on a bus, and there are old parents who still haven't eaten or gone outside their bedrooms. Some houses and apartments have been looted. Some wives are still hysterical. Some husbands are in shock and profound depression. We want to help, but our hands are tied in so many ways. We have to distribute money to some people, and there are legal documents - these things can be done. We have interpreters, but we don't always have the human touch, or maybe the right human touch. We don't want to make mistakes, Mrs. Bhave, and that's why we'd like to ask you to help us."

"More mistakes, you mean," I say.

"Police matters are not in my hands," she answers.

"Nothing I can do will make any difference," I say. "We must all grieve in our own way."

"But you are coping very well. All the people said, Mrs. Bhave is the strongest person of all. Perhaps if the others could see you, talk with you, it would help them."

"By the standards of the people you call hysterical, I am behaving very oddly and very badly, Miss Templeton." I want to say to her, *I wish I could scream, starve, walk into Lake Ontario, jump from a bridge.* "They would not see me as a model. I do not see myself as a model."

I am a freak. No one who has ever known me would think of me reacting this way. This terrible calm will not go away.

She asks me if she may call again, after I get back from a long trip that we all must make. "Of course," I say. "Feel free to call, anytime."

Four days later, I find Kusum squatting on a rock overlooking a bay in Ireland. It isn't a big rock, but it juts sharply out over water. This is as close as we'll ever get to them. June breezes balloon out her sari and unpin her knee-length hair. She has the bewildered look of a sea creature whom the tides have stranded.

It's been one hundred hours since Kusum came stumbling and screaming across my lawn. Waiting around the hospital, we've heard many stories. The police, the diplomats, they tell us things thinking that we're strong, that knowledge is helpful to the grieving, and maybe it is. Some, I know, prefer ignorance, or their own versions. The plane broke into two, they say. Unconsciousness was instantaneous. No one suffered. My boys must have just finished their breakfasts. They loved eating on planes, they loved the smallness of plates, knives, and forks. Last year they saved the airline salt and pepper shakers. Half an hour more and they would have made it to Heathrow.

Kusum says that we can't escape our fate. She says that all those people - our husbands, my boys, her girl with the nightingale voice, all those Hindus, Christians, Sikhs, Muslims, Parsis, and atheists on that plane - were fated to die together off this beautiful bay. She learned this from a swami in Toronto.

I have my Valium.

Six of us "relatives" - two widows and four widowers - choose to spend the day today by the waters instead of sitting in a hospital room and scanning photographs of the dead. That's what they call us now: relatives. I've looked through twenty-seven photos in two days. They're very kind to us, the Irish are very understanding. Sometimes understanding means freeing a tourist bus for this trip to the bay, so we can pretend to spy our loved ones through the glassiness of waves or in sun-speckled cloud shapes.

I could die here, too, and be content.

"What is that, out there?" She's standing and flapping her hands and for a moment I see a head shape bobbing in the waves. She's standing in the water, I, on the boulder. The tide is low, and a round, black, head-sized rock has just risen from the waves. She returns, her sari end dripping and ruined and her face is a twisted remnant of hope, the way mine was a hundred hours ago, still laughing but inwardly knowing that nothing but the ultimate tragedy could bring two women together at six o'clock on a Sunday morning. I watch her face sag into blankness.

"That water felt warm, Shaila," she says at length.

"You can't," I say. "We have to wait for our turn to come."

I haven't eaten in four days, haven't brushed my teeth.

"I know," she says. "I tell myself I have no right to grieve. They are in a better place than we are. My swami says I should be thrilled. My swami says depression is a sign of our selfishness."

Maybe I'm selfish. Selfishly I break away from Kusum and run, sandals slapping against stones, to the water's edge. What if my boys aren't lying pinned under the debris? What if they aren't stuck a mile below that innocent blue chop? What if, given the strong currents ....

Now I've ruined my sari, one of my best. Kusum has joined me, knee-deep in water that feels to me like a swimming pool. I could settle in the water, and my husband would take my hand and the boys would slap water in my face just to see me scream.

"Do you remember what good swimmers my boys were, Kusum?"

"I saw the medals," she says.

One of the widowers, Dr. Ranganathan from Montreal, walks out to us, carrying his shoes in one hand. He's an electrical engineer. Someone at the hotel mentioned his work is famous around the world, something about the place where physics and electricity come together. He has lost a huge family, something indescribable. "With some luck," Dr. Ranganathan suggests to me, "a good swimmer could make it safely to some island. It is quite possible that there may be many, many microscopic islets scattered around."

"You're not just saying that?" I tell Dr. Ranganathan about Vinod, my elder son. Last year he took diving as well.

"It's a parent's duty to hope," he says. "It is foolish to rule out possibilities that have not been tested. I myself have not surrendered hope."

Kusum is sobbing once again. "Dear lady," he says, laying his free hand on her arm, and she calms down.

"Vinod is how old?" he asks me. He's very careful, as we all are. *Is,* not was.

"Fourteen. Yesterday he was fourteen. His father and uncle were going to take him down to the Taj and give him a big birthday party. I couldn't go with them because I couldn't get two weeks off from my stupid job in June." I process bills for a travel agent. June is a big travel month.

Dr. Ranganathan whips the pockets of his suit jacket inside out. Squashed roses, in darkening shades of pink, float on the water. He tore the roses off creepers in somebody's garden. He didn't ask anyone if he could pluck the roses, but now there's been an article about it in the local papers. When you see an Indian person, it says, please give him or her flowers.

"A strong youth of fourteen," he says, "can very likely pull to safety a younger one."

My sons, though four years apart, were very close. Vinod wouldn't let Mithun drown. *Electrical engineering*, I think, foolishly perhaps: this man knows important secrets of the universe, things closed to me. Relief spins me lightheaded. No wonder my boys' photographs haven't turned up in the gallery of photos of the recovered dead. "Such pretty roses," I say.

"My wife loved pink roses. Every Friday I had to bring a bunch home. I used to say, why? After twenty odd years of marriage you're still needing proof positive of my love?" He has identified his wife and three of his children. Then others from Montreal, the lucky ones, intact families with no survivors. He chuckles as he wades back to shore. Then he swings around to ask me a question. "Mrs. Bhave, you are wanting to throw in some roses for your loved ones? I have two big ones left."

But I have other things to float: Vinod's pocket calculator; a half-painted model B-52 for my Mithun. They'd want them on their island. And for my husband? For him I let fall into the calm, glassy waters a poem I wrote in the hospital yesterday. Finally he'll know my feelings for him.

"Don't tumble, the rocks are slippery," Dr. Ranganathan cautions. He holds out a hand for me to grab.

Then it's time to get back on the bus, time to rush back to our waiting posts on hospital benches.

Kusum is one of the lucky ones. The lucky ones flew here, identified in multiplicate their loved ones, then will fly to India with the bodies for proper ceremonies. Satish is one of the few males who surfaced. The photos of faces we saw on the walls in an office at Heathrow and here in the hospital are mostly of women. Women have more body fat, a nun said to me matter-of-factly. They float better.

Today I was stopped by a young sailor on the street. He had loaded bodies, he'd gone into the water when - he checks my face for signs of strength - when the sharks were first spotted. I don't blush, and he breaks down. "It's all right," I say. "Thank you." I had heard about the sharks from Dr. Ranganathan. In his orderly mind, science brings understanding, it holds no terror. It is the shark's duty. For every deer there is a hunter, for every fish a fisherman.

The Irish are not shy; they rush to me and give me hugs and some are crying. I cannot imagine reactions like that on the streets of Toronto. Just strangers, and I am touched. Some carry flowers with them and give them to any Indian they see.

After lunch, a policeman I have gotten to know quite well catches hold of me. He says he thinks he has a match for Vinod. I explain what a good swimmer Vinod is.

"You want me with you when you look at photos?" Dr. Ranganathan walks ahead of me into the picture gallery. In these matters, he is a scientist, and I am grateful. It is a new perspective. "They have performed miracles," he says. "We are indebted to them."

The first day or two the policemen showed us relatives only one picture at a time; now they're in a hurry, they're eager to lay out the possibles, and even the probables.

The face on the photo is of a boy much like Vinod; the same intelligent eyes, the same thick brows dipping into a V. But this boy's features, even his cheeks, are puffier, wider, mushier.

"No." My gaze is pulled by other pictures. There are five other boys who look like Vinod.

The nun assigned to console me rubs the first picture with a fingertip. "When they've been in the water for a while, love, they look a little heavier." The bones under the skin are broken, they said on the first day - try to adjust your memories. It's important.

"It's not him. I'm his mother. I'd know."

"I know this one!" Dr. Ranganathan cries out suddenly from the back of the gallery. "And this one!" I think he senses that I don't want to find my boys. "They are the Kutty brothers. They were also from Montreal." I don't mean to be crying. On the contrary, I am ecstatic. My suitcase in the hotel is packed heavy with dry clothes for my boys.

The policeman starts to cry. "I am so sorry, I am so sorry, ma'am. I really thought we had a match."

With the nun ahead of us and the policeman behind, we, the unlucky ones without our children's bodies, file out of the makeshift gallery.

From Ireland most of us go on to India. Kusum and I take the same direct flight to Bombay, so I can help her clear customs quickly. But we have to argue with a man in uniform. He has large boils on his face. The boils swell and glow with sweat as we argue with him. He wants Kusum to wait in line and he refuses to take authority because his boss is on a tea break. But Kusum won't let her coffins out of sight, and I shan't desert her though I know that my parents, elderly and diabetic, must be waiting in a stuffy car in a scorching lot.

"You bastard!" I scream at the man with the popping boils. Other passengers press closer. "You think we're smuggling contraband in those coffins!"

Once upon a time we were well brought up women; we were dutiful wives who kept our heads veiled, our voices shy and sweet.

In India, I become, once again, an only child of rich, ailing parents. Old friends of the family come to pay their respects. Some are Sikh, and inwardly, involuntarily, I cringe. My parents are progressive people; they do not blame communities for a few individuals.

In Canada it is a different story now.

"Stay longer," my mother pleads. "Canada is a cold place. Why would you want to be all by yourself?" I stay.

Three months pass. Then another.

"Vikram wouldn't have wanted you to give up things!" they protest. They call my husband by the name he was born with. In Toronto he'd changed to Vik so the men he worked with at his office would find his name as easy as Rod or Chris. "You know, the dead aren't cut off from us!"

My grandmother, the spoiled daughter of a rich *zamindar*, shaved her head with rusty razor blades when she was widowed at sixteen. My grandfather died of childhood diabetes when he was nineteen, and she saw herself as the harbinger of bad luck. My mother grew up without parents, raised indifferently by an uncle, while her true mother slept in a hut behind the main estate house and took her food with the servants.

She grew up a rationalist. My parents abhor mindless mortification.

The zamindar's daughter kept stubborn faith in Vedic rituals; my parents rebelled. I am trapped between two modes of knowledge. At thirty-six, I am too old to start over and too young to give up. Like my husband's spirit, I flutter between worlds.

Courting aphasia, we travel. We travel with our phalanx of servants and poor relatives. To hill stations and to beach resorts. We play contract bridge in dusty gymkhana clubs. We ride stubby ponies up crumbly mountain trails. At tea dances, we let ourselves be twirled twice round the ballroom. We hit the holy spots we hadn't made time for before. In Varanasi, Kalighat, Rishikesh, Hardwar, astrologers and palmists seek me out and for a fee offer me cosmic consolations.

Already the widowers among us are being shown new bride candidates. They cannot resist the call of custom, the authority of their parents and older brothers. They must marry; it is the duty of a man to look after a wife. The new wives will be young widows with children, destitute but of good family. They will make loving wives, but the men will shun them. I've had calls from the men over crackling Indian telephone lines. "Save me," they say, these substantial, educated, successful men of forty. "My parents are arranging a marriage for me." In a month they will have buried one family and returned to Canada with a new bride and partial family.

I am comparatively lucky. No one here thinks of arranging a husband for an unlucky widow.

Then, on the third day of the sixth month into this odyssey, in an abandoned temple in a tiny Himalayan village, as I make my offering of flowers and sweetmeats to the god of a tribe of animists, my husband descends to me. He is squatting next to a scrawny *sadhu* in moth-eaten robes. Vikram wears the vanilla suit he wore the last time I hugged him. The *sadhu* tosses petals on a butter-fed flame, reciting Sanskrit mantras and sweeps his face of flies. My husband takes my hands in his.

*You're beautiful,* he starts. Then, *What are you doing here?*

*Shall I stay?* I ask. He only smiles, but already the image is fading. *You must finish alone what we started together.* No seaweed wreathes his mouth. He speaks too fast just as he used to when we were an envied family in our pink split-level. He is gone.

In the windowless altar room, smoky with joss sticks and clarified butter lamps, a sweaty hand gropes for my blouse. I do not shriek. The *sadhu* arranges his robe. The lamps hiss and sputter out.

When we come out of the temple, my mother says, "Did you feel something weird in there?"

My mother has no patience with ghosts, prophetic dreams, holy men, and cults.

"No," I lie. "Nothing."

But she knows that she's lost me. She knows that in days I shall be leaving.

Kusum's put her house up for sale. She wants to live in an ashram in Hardwar. Moving to Hardwar was her swami's idea. Her swami runs two ashrams, the one in Hardwar and another here in Toronto.

"Don't run away," I tell her.

"I'm not running away," she says. "I'm pursuing inner peace. You think you or that Ranganathan fellow are better off?"

Pam's left for California. She wants to do some modelling, she says. She says when she comes into her share of the insurance money she'll open a yoga-cum-aerobics studio in Hollywood. She sends me postcards so naughty I daren't leave them on the coffee table. Her mother has withdrawn from her and the world.

The rest of us don't lose touch, that's the point. Talk is all we have, says Dr. Ranganathan, who has also resisted his relatives and returned to Montreal and to his job, alone. He says, whom better to talk with than other relatives? We've been melted down and recast as a new tribe.

He calls me twice a week from Montreal. Every Wednesday night and every Saturday afternoon. He is changing jobs, going to Ottawa. But Ottawa is over a hundred miles away, and he is forced to drive two hundred and twenty miles a day. He can't bring himself to sell his house. The house is a temple, he says; the king-sized bed in the master bedroom is a shrine. He sleeps on a folding cot. A devotee.

There are still some hysterical relatives. Judith Templeton's list of those needing help and those who've "accepted" is in nearly perfect balance. Acceptance means you speak of your family in the past tense and you make active plans for moving ahead with your life. There are courses at Seneca and Ryerson we could be taking. Her gleaming leather briefcase is full of college catalogues and lists of cultural societies that need our help. She has done impressive work, I tell her.

"In the textbooks on grief management," she replies - I am her confidante, I realize, one of the few whose grief has not sprung bizarre obsessions - "there are stages to pass through: rejection, depression, acceptance, reconstruction." She has compiled a chart and finds that six months after the tragedy, none of us still reject reality, but only a handful are reconstructing. "Depressed Acceptance" is the plateau we've reached. Remarriage is a major step in reconstruction (though she's a little surprised, even shocked, over *how* quickly some of the men have taken on new families). Selling one's house and changing jobs and cities is healthy.

How do I tell Judith Templeton that my family surrounds me, and that like creatures in epics, they've changed shapes? She sees me as calm and accepting but worries that I have no job, no career. My closest friends are worse off than I. I cannot tell her my days, even my nights, are thrilling.

She asks me to help with families she can't reach at all. An elderly couple in Agincourt whose sons were killed just weeks after they had brought their parents over from a village in Punjab. From their names, I know they are Sikh. Judith Templeton and a translator have visited them twice with offers of money for air fare to Ireland, with bank forms, power-of-attorney forms, but they have refused to sign, or to leave their tiny apartment. Their sons' money is frozen in the bank. Their sons' investment apartments have been trashed by tenants, the furnishings sold off. The parents fear that anything they sign or any money they receive will end the company's or the country's obligations to them. They fear they are selling their sons for two airline tickets to a place they've never seen.

The high-rise apartment is a tower of Indians and West Indians, with a sprinkling of Orientals. The nearest bus stop kiosk is lined with women in saris. Boys practice cricket in the parking lot. Inside the building, even I wince a bit from the ferocity of onion fumes, the distinctive and immediate Indianness of frying *ghee*, but Judith

Templeton maintains a steady flow of information. These poor old people are in imminent danger of losing their place and all their services.

I say to her, "They are Sikh. They will not open up to a Hindu woman." And what I want to add is, as much as I try not to, I stiffen now at the sight of beards and turbans. I remember a time when we all trusted each other in this new country, it was only the new country we worried about.

The two rooms are dark and stuffy. The lights are off, and an oil lamp sputters on the coffee table. The bent old lady has let us in, and her husband is wrapping a white turban over his oiled, hip-length hair. She immediately goes to the kitchen, and I hear the most familiar sound of an Indian home, tap water hitting and filling a teapot.

They have not paid their utility bills, out of fear and the inability to write a check. The telephone is gone; electricity and gas and water are soon to follow. They have told Judith their sons will provide. They are good boys, and they have always earned and looked after their parents.

We converse a bit in Hindi. They do not ask about the crash and I wonder if I should bring it up. If they think I am here merely as a translator, then they may feel insulted. There are thousands of Punjabi-speakers, Sikhs, in Toronto to do a better job. And so I say to the old lady, "I too have lost my sons, and my husband, in the crash."

Her eyes immediately fill with tears. The man mutters a few words which sound like a blessing. "God provides and God takes away," he says.

I want to say, but only men destroy and give back nothing. "My boys and my husband are not coming back," I say. "We have to understand that."

Now the old woman responds. "But who is to say? Man alone does not decide these things." To this her husband adds his agreement.

Judith asks about the bank papers, the release forms. With a stroke of the pen, they will have a provincial trustee to pay their bills, invest their money, send them a monthly pension.

"Do you know this woman?" I ask them.

The man raises his hand from the table, turns it over and seems to regard each finger separately before he answers. "This young lady is always coming here, we make tea for her and she leaves papers for us to sign." His eyes scan a pile of papers in the corner of the room. "Soon we will be out of tea, then will she go away?"

The old lady adds, "I have asked my neighbours and no one else gets *angrezi* visitors. What have we done?"

"It's her job," I try to explain. "The government is worried. Soon you will have no place to stay, no lights, no gas, no water."

"Government will get its money. Tell her not to worry, we are honourable people."

I try to explain the government wishes to give money, not take. He raises his hand. "Let them take," he says. "We are accustomed to that. That is no problem."

"We are strong people," says the wife. "Tell her that."

"Who needs all this machinery?" demands the husband. "It is unhealthy, the bright lights, the cold air on a hot day, the cold food, the four gas rings. God will provide, not government."

"When our boys return," the mother says. Her husband sucks his teeth. "Enough talk," he says.

Judith breaks in. "Have you convinced them?" The snaps on her cordovan briefcase go off like firecrackers in that quiet apartment. She lays the sheaf of legal papers on the coffee table. "If they can't write their names, an X will do - I've told them that."

Now the old lady has shuffled to the kitchen and soon emerges with a pot of tea and two cups. "I think my bladder will go first on a job like this," Judith says to me, smiling. "If only there was some way of reaching them. Please thank her for the tea. Tell her she's very kind."

I nod in Judith's direction and tell them in Hindi, "She thanks you for the tea. She thinks you are being very hospitable but she doesn't have the slightest idea what it means."

I want to say, humour her. I want to say, my boys and my husband are with me too, more than ever. I look in the old man's eyes and I can read his stubborn, peasant's message: *I have protected this woman as best I can. She is the only person I have left. Give to me or take from me what you will, but I will not sign for it. I will not pretend that I accept.*

In the car, Judith says, "You see what I'm up against? I'm sure they're lovely people, but their stubbornness and ignorance are driving me crazy. They think signing a paper is signing their sons' death warrants, don't they?"

I am looking out the window. I want to say, *In our culture, it is a parent's duty to hope.*

"Now Shaila, this next woman is a real mess. She cries day and night, and she refuses all medical help. We may have to -"

" - Let me out at the subway," I say.

"I beg your pardon?" I can feel those blue eyes staring at me.

It would not be like her to disobey. She merely disapproves, and slows at a corner to let me out. Her voice is plaintive. "Is there anything I said? Anything I did?"

I could answer her suddenly in a dozen ways, but I choose not to. "Shaila? Let's talk about it," I hear, then slam the door.

A wife and mother begins her new life in a new country, and that life is cut short. Yet her husband tells her: Complete what we have started. We, who stayed out of politics and came halfway around the world to avoid religious and political feuding have been the first in the New World to die from it. I no longer know what we started, nor how to complete it. I write letters to the editors of local papers and to members of Parliament. Now at least they admit it was a bomb. One MP answers back, with sympathy, but with a challenge. You want to make a difference? Work on a campaign. Work on mine. Politicize the Indian voter.

My husband's old lawyer helps me set up a trust. Vikram was a saver and a careful investor. He had saved the boys' boarding school and college fees. I sell the pink house at four times what we paid for it and take a small apartment downtown. I am looking for a charity to support.

We are deep in the Toronto winter, gray skies, icy pavements. I stay indoors, watching television. I have tried to assess my situation, how best to live my life, to complete what we began so many years ago. Kusum has written me from Hardwar that her life is now serene. She has seen Satish and has heard her daughter sing again. Kusum was on a pilgrimage, passing through a village when she heard a young girl's voice, singing one of her daughter's favourite *bhajans*. She followed the music through the squalor of a Himalayan village, to a hut where a young girl, an exact replica of her daughter, was fanning coals under the kitchen fire. When she appeared, the girl cried out, "Ma!" and ran away. What did I think of that?

I think I can only envy her.

Pam didn't make it to California, but writes me from Vancouver. She works in a department store, giving make-up hints to Indian and Oriental girls. Dr. Ranganathan has given up his commute, given up his house and job, and accepted an academic position in Texas where no one knows his story and he has vowed not to tell it. He calls me now once a week.

I wait, I listen, and I pray, but Vikram has not returned to me. The voices and the shapes and the nights filled with visions ended abruptly several weeks ago.

I take it as a sign.

One rare, beautiful, sunny day last week, returning from a small errand on Yonge Street, I was walking through the park from the subway to my apartment. I live equidistant from the Ontario Houses of Parliament and the University of Toronto. The day was not cold, but something in the bare trees caught my attention. I looked up from the gravel, into the branches and the clear blue sky beyond. I thought I heard the rustling of larger forms, and I waited a moment for voices. Nothing.

"What?" I asked.

Then as I stood in the path looking north to Queen's Park and west to the university, I heard the voices of my family one last time. *Your time has come*, they said. *Go, be brave.*

I do not know where this voyage I have begun will end. I do not know which direction I will take. I dropped the package on a park bench and started walking.

▼▼▼▼▼▼▼▼▼

# Acknowledgements

■

Rubicon Publishing Inc. is grateful for the evaluations and suggestions of these educators:

Peter Fanning
Vancouver Board of Education
Vancouver, British Columbia

Douglas Hilker
York Board of Education
Toronto, Ontario

• • • • • • • • • • • • • • • • • • • • • • • • • • • • • • • • • • • • • • • • • • • •

**My Hands:** By Takeo Nakano from *Volvox* (© 1971). Reprinted with permission from Sono Nis Press, Victoria.

**SOJOURNERS**

**Tao Te Ching #80:** By Lao Tzu from *Tao Te Ching*. Translated by Stephen Mitchell. Copyright © 1988 Stephen Mitchell. Reprinted by permission of Harper and Row, Publishers, Inc.

**Exiled From Paradise:** By Eva Hoffman from *Lost in Translation* (© 1989). Reprinted by permission of E. P. Dutton.

**Departure:** By Matilde Gentile Torres from *Italian-Canadian Voices* (© 1984). Reprinted by permission of Mosaic Press.

**The Nun Who Returned to Ireland**:  By Roch Carrier, from *The Hockey Sweater and Other Stories*, translated by Sheila Fischman (Toronto:  House of Anansi Press, 1979).  Reprinted by permission.

## BUILDING ALL OVER AGAIN

**Advice to the Young**:  Reprinted from *Collected Poems* copyright © Miriam Waddington 1986, by permission of Oxford University Press Canada.

**I'm Just Me:  Adrienne Clarkson**:  By Maggie Goh.  Reprinted by permission of the author.

**Black Like Me**:  By Fil Fraser from *Saturday Magazine*, January 1987.  Reprinted by permission of the author.

**Rebirth**:  By Pablo Urbanyi from *Canadian Fiction Magazine*, Vol. 61-62 (1987).  Reprinted by permission of the author.

**A Boat Girl Grows Up**:  By Barry Came from *Maclean's*, July 10, 1989.  Reprinted by permission of Maclean Hunter Limited.

**The Management of Grief**:  From *The Middleman and Other Stories* by Bharati Mukherjee.  Copyright © Bharati Mukherjee, 1988.  Reprinted by permission of Penguin Books Canada Limited.

Every reasonable effort has been made to trace the owners of copyrighted material and to make due acknowledgement.  Any errors or omissions drawn to our attention will be gladly rectified in future editions.